MW01243045

This book reflects the author's present recollections of experiences over time. Some names and characteristics have been changed.

REMEMBER ME

....the raw truth

INTRODUCTION

As far as I can remember, I have always been very cunning and manipulative....

Like when I started school, I can remember feeling like I had to get the attention and I always found myself in the corner or getting a ruler across my ass. Well, that went out the window when I failed the first grade. I tell you that is when life as a manipulator began, first, you must understand that I am a hundred percent (100 %) Momma's boy. When Momma looked at my report card and saw that I failed the first grade, the look she gave me pierced my soul, and from that day until this one she would never have a look of disappointment. Well, at least not because of something that I did.

So, I became the biggest manipulator and bullshitter around. I come from a big family; it was eight of us in the house (4 boys and 4 girls), and we are a very tight family that was taught to always stick together. The neighborhood that I grew up in was a very eventful one. We had everything from the ass whippings from my parents and neighbors. My parents both were from the South, so they were very good parents who had a lot of values, something that was very useful in my life. Like I was saying, I had four sisters and three brothers, plus my niece and nephew who were considered my brother and sister. We lived in West Baltimore in the 1000 block of Lexington Street, the intersection of Lexington and Schroeder where the pool room was located. Boy, I had to be very manipulative because I was very attracted to the pool room, or should I say the people who hung in there.

I had an older brother who I idolized (Johnny) who was slick as my knight and he was a genius at getting money and probably one of the greatest dressers of his time. Johnny had it going on whenever he was home, because of his lifestyle, he gave a lot of time to the State. When I was a jitterbug, I wore my knitted shirts, snake skins, and a wedge heal shoe during my elementary school days. Johnny was one of the best in the country with a million-dollar dream. My brother would always keep me with him, and he would tell me not to let my mother or father know about it.

There was the pool room, as I mentioned before halfway down the block was the Poe Homes and one block from there was Lexington Terrace, and as a little boy, I learned how to survive in the worst circumstances. Half a block in the other direction, this street only consisted of two blocks, was Carlton Street. This is where all my insanity really took off. There were a couple of elementary schools, but the one we attended was #161 Fannie L. Barbour, which was on the corner of Saratoga and Schroeder streets. A lot of my idols hung out on the corners, and I would watch them and everybody knew each other; we were only divided by age, and as we got older, we took different positions. Unknowingly, I became Black because of my complexion, and I was Tyrone Moses' little brother. I loved my brother, but I hated being in his shadow. He set the bar real high for me and Timmy, my ace. No matter what it was Tyrone could do it, but fighting was his shit. Oh, by the way in my hood, you better know how to fight. We didn't use weapons; we fist to cuff. In my house that's all we did was wrestle and challenge each other girls included. My father got a thrill out of watching until he said, "Stop," and he was only saying it once. Daddy was a big dude who didn't take any shit. He worked hard at the Chemical Company, and he was a great provider. What my uncles would tell me was he was just like Tyrone when he was younger. I have five uncles (my father's brothers). Back to Carlton Street, these two blocks you could get whatever you were looking for. Everything happened on Carlton Street, so I had the pool room and the Poe Homes in one direction. Fast forward to about the fourth grade, I'm the biggest manipulator in the school; so of course, I outgrew my age group and now I'm cutting out of school and going to hang out in the Poe Homes, smoking cigarettes and then the alcohol (booze) came. Man did I love the taste of booze, or should I say the feeling it gave me. Now I would get alcohol from Aunt Willis Mae (Momma's only sister) who lived in New York. I would hang around my favorite uncle Esau, who was my main man. Boy, everyone should have an Uncle Esau. I was his right-hand man as well; and like Johnny, he was a sharp dresser and a straight ladies' man, so if the lady had a daughter, it was on. Well, the year was 1970 and I'm learning how to get the business started. Johnny just brought the restaurant (Greasy Spoon) on Lexington and Schroeder, right across from the pool room. He made me feel like I was really running things. Soon as I got out of school, I went to the restaurant, and Slim who was the cook would make me a T-bone steak (still my favorite today), and me and my cousin Junior who we called Slap because he was pretty fast with his hands. I remember the day somebody was talking a lot of shit and out of nowhere Tyrone told Junior to step to the person and from that day forward we called him Slap Young (he preferred just Slap). This took place on Carlton Street, so he got plenty of respect; as for myself and Timmy, we had to get out of Tyrone's shadow and build our reputation. That didn't go so well because if you were beefing with Timmy, you were beefing with Anky; so, I guess we were twins, and still until this day, they call me Timmy and

I still answer. Everyone needs to have a Timmy in their life. I will say that about all of my siblings, we were close as any family. I remember going out with Ms. Stell, she was the lady in west Baltimore who sold the Afro or that's what I thought, and I felt bad when I was stealing all the change I could put in my shoes. I had to hide it, but Timmy and Poop (my sister, one year older) who is very good with her hands, but the prettiest black in the neighborhood would have a ball with the stolen money. Going on Ms. Stell's paper route, I fell in love with Pennsylvania Avenue, another place I got familiar with while hanging out with Johnny. Back then Sampson's was the best restaurant on the east coast. People would come from all over to eat at Sampson's. He was a big deal in Baltimore, known as Black Johnny, and he had associated with the who's who of Baltimore and New York. The avenue was lit up and the lifestyle was very attractive to me. I used to have a club house in a vacant house, like an apartment; we had to have some place to go and sneak and do our thing. I used to watch the older guys in the hood go in and they would cook up and shoot dope, and what I saw after they finished was so attractive. I'm between 11 and 13 and this clubhouse was a place to sniff glue and smoke all the things that were off limit in my house.

Anyway, my brother was home staying with us, straight out of jail, and he was making some checks and had a girlfriend who he told me to keep her warm while he handled his business (my real experience.) I always had a girl in the clubhouse a fast one of course, I played "7-11 and catch one, catch-all," which were always an opportunity to "get a little bit," but this was a grown lady. I was big and always more advanced than my age group, but man, I fell in love. She told me to "strip," dam, I still remember that and from that point moving forward it was not a joke, which makes me think of my first real love. She lived on Carlton Street, she had five sisters and no brothers, and she was my first real girl. By this time, I'm in the world still trying to get my own identity. I was in our block and Timmy was within eyesight now, we were smoking weed, taking pills, and it's all about the "monkey hustle." Everybody had a hustle, and I had several by now. I'm going to Harlem Park Junior High School, always sharp and a pocket full of weed (nickel bags.) Now Momma got sick, when I was in the 7th grade, of course, I failed because all my time was at the hospital with Momma, and I couldn't focus. Johnny came home again, and he told me to get my act together and Momma got better. I was so manipulative and had so many female friends that while in school, I got extra assignments that they helped me do and I got put back in my right grade. That summer Johnny was cleaning out a new store on Whitlock Street and we were going to burn shit down. I went to New York for a couple of weeks and in the process, Johnny was killed. He got his million-dollar dream, but it was the death of him. Aunt Willie Mae and I were in Baltimore within hours. We could not get the right information, I was ready to commit murder, needless to say; we never opened the store, and I got into it with a fucking FBI Agent. He said some dumb shit like "he was a guy we have been trying to catch off guard for some years."

Life got difficult after my brother was killed and I was out of control. I remember one fight where I had the whole neighborhood's attention and Tyrone told me "You better whip his ass or I'm going to whip your ass" and Timmy sided with Tyrone; but I had no fear, fighting was a pastime of mine and I was really demonstrating on his older brother. Afterward, we all squashed the beef and dudes bought Wild Irish Rose, Thunderbird, and plenty of beer. He became a good friend and from that, I became a person not to be fucked with. I tell you my hood there were all types, but I chose to be with the crowd most likely to end up in jail. I was only 14 when Billy and I figured it out. I believe he was a year or two older, but anybody I hung out with was at least 3 years older than I was, so I wore a lot of masks. At 16, the summer came, and I worked a summer job, again Momma made that happen because she was the neighborhood mother and she was well loved; but it was nothing compared to the money I was making off the hustle; but if Momma wanted me to do it, I did it, point blank. I loved my mother to no end, so I had to wear another mask. Another friend called me Face, he was a few years older than us all, but when Billy and I figured things out, we would start the business, and selling weed was okay. All the big shots were selling smack, gee, or boogie, which where are all street names for dope, so we came up with a plan. We got on the Trailways Bus to "New York, "here we come!" I knew how to get from 42nd Street to Brooklyn and Nostrand Avenue was the strip and I had met a dude named Fonze. I would steal and rob people with him while I was up there for one of many vacations. Fonze knew where the good shit was. Billy and I would make a couple of trips and of course, we had to have had some good shit because each time all 10 of our bundles or 2 would be gone in like 2 days. I was still going to Harlem Park and the dudes from Mount and Mosher Street were thick, who had a crew from Gilmore Homes, Murphy Homes, and the Terrace; and my crew #161, Saratoga and Schroeder. By now, Daddy and Momma had purchased a brand-new house at 318 N. Carey Street, it wasn't that far from Carrollton Avenue, and I could see that things were getting real. As I continue to remember when I was in the 7th grade, Johnny being killed execution style. At that time, I was in New York, and I was now ready to become a business owner as Johnny had a storefront on Whitelock Street and it was going to be in my name. Johnny was very smart, so I asked him while we were cleaning out the spot, why would we want to open a store here and one down the street? Johnny said he had already had that figured out too. He simply said, he has insurance and he said he was going to be detained for a short while and Junior and I were going to burn the competition down and I was impressed and ready to make it happen. Johnny had a million-dollar goal and in the process of getting the million, it cost him his life, and the money was stolen Johnny's best friend was mad and so was I. For the first time with all the insane shit I had done and doing, I realized that I was capable of murder and now I feel like the world owed me and somebody had to pay. I went on a senseless binge that everybody was a victim of, and I started using syrup, doritins, window pain, bladder, and mickey mouse (these were acids). This took you out of your mind, and I would have a beer no matter where I was or what I was doing became my trademark. I sniffed quickie, took Elavil, dummies, xmas tree, and valiums. When I took valiums, I would be in a blackout and some would tell me what I had done the next day, it was about everything goes. I became very manipulative and still had to please Momma. So, that summer I would make excuses to get off work and then I figured that I would have the supervisor so afraid of me that I ran the crew and we would really wild out, there were 5 of us. We worked, hustled together, and we signed in together and kept going the next year. I went back to school, and I could steal and for the most, that's what I would do. It was in the summer and designer jeans hit the school, and I was on top of things and very feared by many, but when they say good girls love bad guys believe it, because I had at least 3 main girls and my rap game was tight. Bill came home, by this time he had a daughter, and he was the best at his trade. I was called Theo. I had a girl who was wise with her hustle, and she would take money. Her hustle was on point, and she made sure I was good she would line my pockets and bring bags of clothes. She wanted to go further but what turned her on was a good ass whooping. She liked it so I started treating all the girls like that. So now beating my girlfriends because I think it's cool and I'm getting fucked up every day. Now we got to get this money so we can go get another package. Whiz said, "we need a big score," because he knows about us taking trash cans from work and wheeling them into G.C. Murphy. We took the merchandise and I told them, "To load the cans." And when they got to the front where the security guard was, is when my turn came. I would put the guard in the L and they would walk out. We ran through a couple of guards like that, but Whiz said, "it was petty and we still had to sell the shit," so he told me, "That we need to take money bags." I said, "fuck it, let's do it. I said, "to rob a bank we need guns," but that wasn't what Whiz had in mind. He had already started going downtown to what we called the loop, and he was scoping out the store owners to see which banks they were getting their daily operational money and how. While I was in school, Whiz was scheming and he had them down the pack, but he was only comfortable with me. We would need at least one more person, so we got Bob (Shank) in on it with us, and we went each day just as he said, and he was smart. He had different store owners and different banks for three weeks. We robbed them and not one time did we use a gun. I wasn't that good at clipping or creeping, but enforcer was my shit. I would put them in an L headlock and Bob was my lookout and Whiz would get each pocket and the money bag. Whiz was fast as lightning, and he ran with the money. Bob had to distract the person after I slung them to the ground to give me a little leeway and I ran, but once we made it to the project, then Whiz was smiling, and I trusted him, so I knew the money was right. We did that and we were getting it. Whiz took care of his daughter, and I kept a stash. I still couldn't do things because what if my father found out? Now my brother, whom we call Tim Black, was known for one and done, he had a power punch and ran with Top, who was well known too, and he could creep. So, I didn't want to hustle with my brother because I didn't want my parents to say I got him into this lifestyle; but his reputation became bigger, and they would even pay Tim Black to handle situations for them. They were "Big Shots." This was the beginning of some crazy times. We were now going up to New York with more money and getting a lot more products. We were getting 2 bundles of P Funk; a bundle of Tow was thirty bucks and we started bringing back bundles of tens and renamed it. The first ones we called "Fire." It sold like hot cakes, but I started to notice Whiz had changed. He didn't want any wine, no pills, no syrup or doritins. All he would do was drink soda and maybe smoke some weed. Whiz ran the stash house that we paid an older dude, who use to mess with Whiz's sister. It was a familiar look, but I just couldn't put my hands on what it was, but it looked familiar. We kept jamming and we had another batch and called it Hell, and man that shit had the addicts chasing and my name was ringing really loud. I had to always be awake for the fact that everyone knew Miss Ora. She was one of the most liked ladies in this whole city, so it really made it hard for me to keep shit away from her. This was my reason for having so many names because I was always trying to please my mother, ever since she gave me that look after failing the first grade. My cover-up was my cousin Junior, we were also cool, but he really wasn't with half of the shit I was into; and if he was my justification, he didn't have to because at the end of the day he had just as much as I had, and that was my mother's boy. I still believe that he was probably telling but I lived several lives with so much ease that when someone would tell her I had committed a crime or had beaten someone senseless, Momma would always say, "not my Anky, y'all got him confused." I would do anything to please my mother, so most of the time she thought I was working the summer job and after school, down at one of the recreation centers. I was just 14 years old, and I had already created a monster so many people were afraid, and the old ladies would say shit like "at the rate you're going you won't live to see sixteen," so I had to get all my living done now. We are on Carey Street, and it was kind of easy to get away with shit because most of these people were homeowners and they had no idea that it was me and my crew breaking into houses. I had learned one thing from Billy and that was how to scheme and set up a situation. I had taken so many of the houses in the block that I started feeling sorry for them because they didn't have as much as I thought they had. So, I chilled in the block and started to get to know some of the people, but they all knew something about me from school or just watched me come and go. Now when we left Lexington Street, Uncle Esau got himself a room, and that is when I met Esau, Jr. He was a New Jersey slick and was older, but we clicked because like I had been saying to everyone, I hung out with was at least 3 years older than me, but he fucked up when he stole from Uncle and locked him in the apartment. I was Uncle Esau main man, and he was mine, but he told me to let that go, and I did. I swear, me and Uncle Esau, I called him Joe, he moved to the 500 block of Carrollton Avenue, so there was another spot for me to check out. On Carey Street, we had an Afro lean Block and I had flipped tires inside and out, painted my mother's front and everything was matching, and this lady came out of nowhere and said, "this is the boy that put my son in the hospital, he did it." My mother jumped up and once again said, "I don't know who you're talking about, you got my son confused with, but he isn't nothing like that, so don't come pointing the finger at him." Word had got back that something was going to "jump off" at the block party, so me and my

crew were ready; but it turns out that Archie

had challenged somebody to a dance-off.

See, we settled a lot of little bullshit beefs with

dance-offs, it was Wolries Barn, The Capri,

32nd Street, or the Carousel. I was the

youngest out of this crew and Archie took me

to the Carousel. He went heads up with a

nigger from Cherry Hill. The dude was on it,

but Archie was tall and slim and when

everybody looked around, Archie was spinning

around and broke out into some serious water

gating. So, I can get down, but not like Archie.

I would normally jump out for my crew and

then some of the others would get busy, this

Thursday night at the Capri. Some eastside dudes that I had taken some of their shit when we were down the Loop, came at me dead wrong, Tim Black, Curley, Blue and Bob Shank, Hank, and some other dudes from the hood were all there. But you know me, I told his crew to just let me and slim go outside and handle our business or we could all just go at it. So, Roger, one of the older dudes from East, recognized me from selling him and his friends some shit we took from the Hecht Company and must have had some clout over east because he told his crew to keep it going and he and Curley would go out and make sure the fight was fair. Tim Black was having an anxiety attack; he couldn't just let it go and let me go heads up because me and Timmy were one. But I begged him to calm down. I told him I would be back in a minute and true to my word, I was back. I learned to use my elbow as a dangerous weapon, so with one elbow to the temple, the fight was over for now. They were fucked up with the fact that it went down the way it did, so we had an all-out rumble and at that time no one had a gun or just wasn't being used; only fist fight, but that would soon change. I remember once, when Johnny came home and he and Archie were scheming something, and they were making it happen on Edmondson and Calhoun, just up the street from the Club Astoria. I was now hanging out during the day after school selling shit in 161 parks and the evening with Junior, who we were now calling Slap. Now a couple of weeks later Johnny was killed execution style, that's when I knew that I could murder someone, but Archie had become close with Johnny, and he knew how much I meant to Johnny. Archie was a hustler who was very skilled as a pickpocket and loved to dress. He would give me some of his clothes because he was about to head off to Senior High School. But what Archie didn't know was I was selling dope, hustling, and robbing people regularly, but I loved to dress, and boy could I put it on.

We were getting better at our hustles, and Curley was a master. We were hitting Gage's and Johnnie favorite Bernard Hills. I had graduated from the 9th and graduated to the 10th grade and Slap came out of the 12th grade. Uncle Esau let us have a house party at his spot. He was quite a ladies' man, and I had a key to his house; I told you I was his ace. Everyone came to the party, and I had about 4 girls who all felt they were my main girl, so I just played like the host, and didn't pay either of them much attention. The next day, Uncle Esau told me to go and meet his other son at the Trailways Station downtown, so I said, "sure enough." I said, "is he expecting me?" My uncle said, "no, he is expecting me, but don't worry, you will know him when you see him. Now Uncle Esau always talked about this son, we all knew his daughter Janice, but this was the younger son. I told him, "I hope he doesn't try that shit that Esau Jr. did. We just laughed, and I grabbed a can of his Pabst Blue Ribbon, and downtown I went. The bus from Newark pulled in just as Uncle Esau said. I recognized Vincent straight from the start, I saw a real easy victim getting off the bus, but I could take no chances, so I introduced myself, and he had on a patchwork shirt, nothing that I would ever wear. What stuck out was this little dude had a box of

Newport's in his shirt pocket and I thought to myself, all the shit I be doing and getting drugs, you name it, and still hiding my cigarettes from my parents. Plus, we were either Kools or Salem smokers, but hell I asked for a smoke and then we headed uptown. I stopped at Sampson's and got us some rolls and gravy; he wanted to be sure it was no pork in it. He was like all the New Jersey Muslims. As we got further up the street to Fayette and Carrollton, we were back in the hood. I spotted this really pretty girl. She was eating a dream sickle ice cream and I said to her, "you sure make that ice cream look good and I sure would like some." She said, "I know who you are. Your name is Anky, but I hear people call you other names and hear you're a bad person." I was stunned not at what she was saying, but the fact I didn't know her. In my hood, I knew everyone, but she said they moved to live with her grandmother on Fayette Street. She told me, "You don't have to take my ice cream, I will buy you one." I said, "No, I want that one in your hand." She smiled and then gave me her ice cream. Then she went to Mr. Richard's and bought herself another one. I told her that she was going to belong to me. She said, "she wasn't going to belong to nobody," but her smile was saying something different. That day I met two of the most important people in my life, but I also had to add an extra ego. Those two would call me Anky. Now as time went on Vincent told us he would prefer Eugene instead of Vincent. He was catching on fast, but there is no way that I can get him mixed up in all the shit I was into. But, at the end of the day, when it was time to chill, I would go get Eugene and we would go to Fayette Street. After all, he knew Bernadette as well as I did, we all met the same day. Now just like his dad, Eugene had a way with the ladies and soon met Denise who was friends with Bernadette. We all started hanging out together. Bernadette left Harlem Park because she moved, and she went to Lake Clifton. I was fifteen and had shit going on still in high school; and this summer, Whiz, and Rod Shank had the park-wide open. As we got low on supplies, I went to get more shit and it all started to make some of what was different about Whiz. He and T were in the house and when I opened the door, it felt like it was back at the old clubhouse. I saw hypodermic needles and a spoon. "T" was putting the needle in Whiz's arm and just that fast, I knew what was going on. They tried to hide shit out of respect. Whiz told me he just didn't want me to start shooting up because he felt I could stay in school and become something and get out of the hood. I told Whiz

"Man fuck that shit, we boys and wanted to try it." I told him how I would watch the old guys from the clubhouse. Whiz said, "he knew I had the clubhouse, and that was the only reason he never went in the shooting gallery in the old house." I told him we do everything together and he was only a couple of years older than me. He said, "it was up to me, but he would not be the first person to help me get on." He left with the bundles to take to the park, and I told him that I wanted to try it. "T," said, "Hell no man, I have too much respect for your older brother, and if he was living, he would have me killed for that." I told "T," consider this the last time you got some of our shit. We would find somewhere else to stash our shit and he could forget today's pay." He quickly changed his tune and said, "This shit y'all got will kill you, so I will give you this type." I stuck my arm out and my life would never be the same again. Also, I would never need anyone to hit me again, it was simple. We were young, I just turned fifteen, met my dream girl, met Vincent, and was getting money. Theo was my name all during my high school. Whiz had got jammed and because of his record at seventeen, he went to the Maryland Penitentiary with 5 years. I was loyal, did what I could for him to help with his daughter, and visited him, which became an omen. I was now stealing cars from the port and keeping them for a while, and then abandoned them. I noticed that my man who put me down was keeping the cars not hiding or anything. I couldn't do that; my parents could not find out about anything I was doing. I realized that all the papers were in the cars, and no one was looking for them; so, what can I do? I found a salvage yard that would give me money for the cars on the second sale. He tried to set me up. He got caught trying to sell the cars as is instead of taking the parts and selling them. I saw the feds in his garage at the time we were supposed to be making a deal. So, I left the car, and when I didn't show up, they round another car, and locked his ass up. When he came home, I kicked his ass for trying me! Whiz came home and wanted to get a quick hit, so he scooped out the Hecht Company. He had it to a tee and all we had to do is the same thing that we had done for 2 nights. We stayed hidden until the store was closed, and then we cleaned up. Whiz had taken order; Tony was the fence and Carly hooked us up. We spent the night taking all the good shit and at 6:00 a.m., just like Whiz said, at the door to the alley we heard a click. We had 4 bags each and we were out with all that shit. It was all over the news that Hecht Company was robbed, but they didn't have any suspects and didn't know how it was done, but we had better sense than to do that shit again. Whiz started taking jewelry. The boy was smooth. I was a shame. All I had to do was keep the people's attention and I told Whiz that no matter what, I would never let them lock the doors on him. Shit, he was so smooth, I would be looking for him and he would slide out from the back of the store, and I knew he had made it out. Whiz and I were always true to each other, and he told me that we were getting too well known in this town. He told me he was going to go to Hollywood with a crew of jewel thieves. While Whiz was gone, my addiction started to take off. I was known around town

for sticking up dealers, but I had one problem,
I never hid from anyone. I couldn't because
Anky was a student who sold weed, but
Blackface was a low life. Now with a price
over his head, at the time I was going to
Southwestern, and Tim Black and Bob Shank
were locked up.

The word was Tim Black was looking out for the dude who had the hit on me; little brother over the jail, so we came to an agreement that we would squash shit and he owe Tim Black for taking care of his brother. Tim really liked the little dude, and the dude was catching big time. So as luck would have it, I was locked up for an assault on a police officer. That was another thing the police couldn't lock me up, not just one or two of them, I would fight them real hard, so I was arrested for fighting them. When I got over the jail, a couple of old friends were the guards, and then when I hit receiving, Tim Black sent me a package. We were all on section Eagle Village for the hoppers and then we had to go to chase all that, but we weren't going anywhere. My mother somehow got my charges dropped. She had a bunch of people willing to say that I was being harassed. Timmy had to fight his charges and eventually beat it because Daddy paid for a lawyer. Daddy would do anything for us, but he wasn't visiting anybody in jail. I went back to school, and it was because the teacher really didn't know me, they thought my name was Theodore and Anthony was doing all the work. Bernadette was smart and I had a couple of other girls helping with my work, and if I was good at anything with all the bull shit, lying, and scheming since I was twelve, was how to manipulate. Even with that, I was always a smart dude, who just wanted to please his mother. By now, I am in the tenth heading for the eleventh grade, and now it was about how many credits I had and what classes would be needed to graduate. I had to give my mother the pleasure of attending my graduation, despite everyone else counting me out, she never gave up on me and I would get this diploma, cap, and gown, the whole nine. The summer came and this must have been the craziest summer ever, but I would be heading back to school to start the eleventh grade now. I had to do it for two people, my mother, now my girl; and wanted to show the town that they were wrong. I must admit I was a beast in the streets and now it was me and Tim Black and a couple of his friends selling coke and dope. Now not only was I shooting smack, but I was also hooked on a speedball. Eugene was back for the summer, and we became so tight that I was stopping in New Jersey on weekends. Things in the hood were still crazy. I was still robbing, stealing, and selling drugs was no more fun without my crew. I just didn't want Timmy to know that I was shooting up, so I went on my own. I stuck up a guy that was selling for Timmy, and he heard about it and that was the first time that we went heads up against each other in public. My brother told me if you are a friend and need something, you could just ask. I went to Fayette Street and was told that they were some guys threatening my girl about my whereabouts. So, I immediately went looking for whoever those guys were, and it turned out that it was somebody that I had robbed, and they had a crew looking for me. It was said, "they are strapped carrying guns." My man Blue got word of it and came looking for me after I ran into a shop and he said, "Fuck them niggas and those bitches with guns, which made them dangerous. To my surprise, he had some guns and he had planned to get the ups on them and that's just what we did. Shoap went up to them because they were looking for me and he put the gun to the dude's head that had all the mouth and then I came with mine. We took their guns, and I told the dude we do things a little different than they do. So, I told them to be fair and let it be known that Shoap has nothing to do with what was about to happen. I first beat him with the gun and then told him to run for his life; meanwhile, all of his friends were pleading and saying "man we don't want no more trouble. I told Shoap to leave, but he said, "We stand together," so I told the crew, five of them to run and pray I let them get a little way before I begin shooting. I was now always strapped. I was glad my girl's mother moved to Cedonia because shit was really getting heavy. We never were supposed to involve women and children in any shit that took place in the streets, that was a code and they had violated it. So, now one would stand with them once the truth came out, but it made me even more dangerous because what if someone wanted me and went after my mom, that was again the thought of possible murder. So, I tried my best to stay on the low, it was more about doing shit outside of the neighborhood. I went that summer doing things as if I would be what they were saying about me. I thought because I had been so malicious, people said I would not live to the age of sixteen. I was going to school and only needed six credits. The only problem was 2 Math classes, 2 English classes, an American History and 1 elective which would be swimming, first period for 2 years and 3 months for my twelfth grade. I got word that Whiz had gotten locked up in another state, but it wasn't any problem, he was built tough and could do time. I was hustling with some of the guys from school and both years I carried around a brown briefcase that contained my book about a hundred bags of weed and a little 25 automatic, and I kept a bunch of girls around me. My girl was over east at Lake Clifton, and she was still making sure I was on top of my grades. I had promised that I would take her to my twelfth-grade prom, so she stayed on top of me, and as I said, I was no dummy. Now Momma was hearing more and more about some of the things that I was doing. She was convinced when Daddy called me in the room and told me that "he was really good at minding his business." And he said, "you might have your mother fooled, but I heard you say something out your mouth giving Timmy some advice." But from what he heard, the things that people were saying were true and if I don't stop using drugs and shooting guns, somebody was going to kill me. My father was as wise as he had told me plain and simple that "I was one person harming so many people and that people don't forget when someone harms them" and then he said, "you might not remember all the people you harm, but all these people must only remember one person that did them harm." That hit me in the gut, but I was already out there, although it was all recreational. Until one day when I couldn't seem to figure out, what was going on with me. I was talking to "T" and he said, "Man you're ill." I said, "what the fuck are you talking about." And he said it again, "man you're ill, and he then said, Come on." We went to his house, and he cooked up and sure enough, I was feeling good. All the sick shit was gone and then for a second time, he said "I hate this shit, but man you got a habit." I wasn't any damn fool, and I knew just what he was saying to me and that really unleashed a beast. We had eighteen-month jobs now and I only had to be in school until eleven o'clock and I would sell enough weed. That was slow money and I liked nice shit and made sure my girl had nice shit also. Now Eugene was finishing school this year and was still seeing Denise and in New Jersey, but he made up his mind that after graduation he was coming to Baltimore to live. That was the agreement he had with his dad. Bernadette was having her junior prom, so I went with her.

Then the summer came, and she was just not feeling it, so she ran away and stayed with her grandmother on Fayette Street and Momma got her a summer job. I was still doing my thing, but I always heard my father telling me "All they must remember is you." I'll be damned! One night we all were chilling over in Franklin Square; we were deep, everybody was talking about what club to hit, and suddenly out of nowhere, this guy jumps out of his car and out of the crowd, he points his rifle right at me because he didn't want anybody but me. Tim Black was with us, and most people got us confused, we can pass for twins, but this guy came right for me, and I was running for my life. I ran to the opposite side of my house, where there was a stable and they must have been working back there. I fell face down in the ditch and all I heard were pellets from the rifle going over my head. I bounced up before he could reload and ran up Mulberry to the alley of my house. I ran into the doghouse and called Shoap to hide me. I could hear him saying, "I know your back her, and I'm going to kill your black ass." By this time, I could hear the helicopter flying over the area, and police was everywhere. From that I heard, this dude wanted me so bad that he kept looking for me and he got arrested. It was for the first time in my life I was afraid and all I could hear was daddy saying, "they only have to remember one person." They had to "remember me." Word got out that the gunman was after me and I saw a look on Momma's face that was almost as bad as when I failed the first grade. That look that I swore I wouldn't make her have, my fear was gone, and I was trying to figure out my next move. So, I went to get my girl who was crying, and she was saying "what are you getting yourself into."

Uncle Esau, me, and Eugene, who is now Box, were now officially a part of the crew and had so much love for me, but he said, "that was crazy, I had a good girl, and doing good in school." I decided the next year would be my last. If I could survive the streets and had to beat the odds, because I was sixteen turnings seventeen in March, but the truth was shit but really hectic. Now I wanted to do better for myself, and Bernadette, she told me that she loved me and wanted to have my baby. I had a couple of offers to have a child, but this was the one and we set out to make it a reality, because I wanted a son. I would have her hook school and meet me at 534, then I would go to Mr. Rob's and get me a couple of quarts and she did like beer, but a little. She would drink and smoke a little weed and then we would set up and make our baby. She thought that would slow me down. Although she did get pregnant, and her mother hated me for that; I mean hated me. I wasn't the type of guy that someone wanted for their child, and she hated me, but Bernadette didn't. We truly loved each other. I got locked up that summer for some dumb shit; this time I was on Steel side W-section, which was the section most West Baltimore dudes went from M & N. I was still shooting dope, so I was greeted with a roll from the toilet paper with a set of work and some smack to take off the "willies." I told my mom to let me stay for two weeks before she paid the bail; she and Bernadette didn't know why I would ask them to do such a thing. Timmy told them that it was just time for me to think about the way my life was going, he was covering for me. I told him I wanted to dry out (detox), so I sat for 16 days, and all the charges were dropped because nobody was willing to show up or press charges in the streets, because shit got handled in the streets. Word had gotten to them somehow that I had some serious dudes from Pennsylvania Avenue area who were going to kill me; I went to Brunt Street to find them before they got the ups on me. I stole a car and went over there and waited until I saw them in a crowd shooting dice. The urge to rob the dice game hit me, but I was there for another reason. I exposed myself and asked, "Who was looking for Black," and before I knew it, gunshots started, so I was returning fire, and I know for a fact I hit 2 of them. I don't know the outcome because I got in the car came in and left. I left the car at Lafayette Square and went to Uncle Esau house as if nothing happened. I never heard any more from those dudes and all I could hear was my father saying, "All they have to remember is you." I was lying low and would be coming out of school if I could make just one more year. Eugene had joined the Army. His dad told him to go and make something of himself, and there was a recruiter who came to my house. Eugene, my high school buddy was going in on the delayed entry program, but my record was not the best, but it was still juvenile shit. So, my mother, the one person that would have told me to jump off a building, and I would've trusted it, would not hurt me; that's the one person I loved the most and wanted to please. She suggested that I go into the service straight out of high school and my girlfriend said we would start a life together.

My father thought it was the only hope I had, so I signed on the dotted line. They got my record straight and were checking on me. My thoughts were "where I should have the summer as my big party." My son was born in June, but to be honest with you, I was supposed to be there, but her mother didn't contact me. I was in the streets, but for some reason, this summer was different, we did go to prom. That New Year's we were together, and it dawned on me that I would be going into the Military in September of 1979. I spent all the time with Bernadette because we both knew that in June both of our lives would be changing, and we were hoping it was going to be for the best. That New Year's Eve would be different from all the rest. My mother and Bernadette had already planned how my New Year's Eve would be. It wouldn't be at a club or somewhere getting revenge or having someone get revenge on me. I would be with Bernadette bringing the new year in, but that didn't go so well either. There was never a reason for me to carry a real gun around my girl and gunplay wasn't that type of beef, but her mother got so many of those warm Colt 45s and a couple of valiums in her, and all hell broke loose. I had to force her little good girl to go against her wishes. When the baby comes, she's going to raise the baby, so

Bernadette can have a life. Her boyfriend, Harry and I were always cool, he was a guard over the jail. He started talking about her and I am moving and some of the shit that he heard about me. This "mutha fucker" pulled out his gun and asked me, "do you have yours?" He went nuts on me talking about how dangerous I was, and they weren't sure in their home because I was the type that people would kill my family to get to me, all types of shit now. Bernadette and her brother Raymond knew that this dude was dead wrong. So, Bernadette must've called my mother because when I looked up, my sister, Poop, who loved me to life, was out there to get me; but we weren't leaving without Bernadette. She was still arguing with her mom and Shaky, that was his nickname because he was really an alcoholic and would shake if he didn't get a drink. I was boiling and Blackface had emerged. Uncle Esau told me to bring Bernadette over to his house and he was going to stay with his lady, so we could have his place because pregnant or not, the only person sleeping with a woman in 318 was Moses and Ora, as far as they knew about, but the night ended up pretty good. Now I haven't said much to Momma yet, but I will tell you that they fucked up and I knew it. But we had a good summer, I would say, and was getting close to my time to go in. I would have that summer and when school started in September, I was on my way to Fort Jackson, South Carolina, but could I make it until September? To my surprise, Tim Black didn't want to see this shit. He was in the Air National Guard and had done basic training. Everyone did all they could do to keep me off the streets, so I would make it to September, and I did calm down a lot. I walked across the stage and both my parents and Bernadette were there. I was "fucked up;" I almost slept my turn, if someone hadn't hit me and said, "that's you." I got my diploma and there was a big roar, hand clapping and yelling, "yeah, you did it, you did it!" That summer was far the hardest. I was trying to get my mind right and didn't want to get ill while in basic, so I kicked my dope habit cold turkey, and it was simply nothing. I wanted to stop, and I stopped. I spent most of the summer at 534 Carrollton Avenue, and when Bernadette wasn't there, I had company. I was "hot shit" to all these girls; a couple was my sister's friends. Bernadette's mother was really making shit hard for her, which meant it was hard for me and I didn't like it one fucking but she was mom. She promised Bernadette after I got my shit straight, her and Anthony Jr. would be coming to live with me whenever I was stationed. I was going to do the whole twenty years and she could go to college and things would all work out just fine. So, the summer was still like always, my friends were my friends, and I didn't tell them that I was even going, so I had to continue with the regular routines. I wasn't shooting any smack, but I was a benign kind of guy, and I still took syrup and dortins whenever I wanted to have a good nod, that was always my thing, just a good speedball. I was still robbing people like mad, but for some reason, all the excitement was gone, the thrill of the take was just not there, so I just started going to clubs and that's when some shit jumped off that the 32nd Street

Plaza, that was an eastside club, but shit I never cared for. I went all over the city. I had to just keep my mother from hearing about some of the things that I was doing and 32nd Street was on Greenmount Avenue, a popular strip in East Baltimore. It was a Saturday night and the only person who wanted to hang out was my man, Blue. We called him Shoap, bow down and he was a true friend. He was the only person who hung in there when we left #161 and was sent to Booker T. Washington. He went back-to-back with me no matter what. Anyway, somebody the Shoap knew from hanging out downtown on the block gave Shoap a heads up that there was a plot against us, and we were going to be ambushed when we left the club again, over something that I had done to somebody. This was a situation, but fear wasn't a part of our style, so Shoap told me what was going on, but we would be outnumbered and that would be the only way that would come out on top. We had a stolen car that was parked about a block away from the club, but getting to the car would be a challenge, so I started looking around the club to see who it could be, but I had wronged so many people that wasn't going to happen and again all I heard was my dad saying "You won't remember everyone you harmed, but all they had to remember is you." I wasn't afraid and I figured I would at least take somebody out of the bunch and beat him even while I was getting jumped. It was not going to be simple I told Shoap to let them focus on me and just go and get the car. Shoap asked, "are you crazy"? He said, "we don't do that, we roll together." I noticed Shoap didn't seem to be as worried about what was about to happen; but I braced myself, got myself a drink, and said, "fuck it, let's just see what happens." We always had a thing in our crew, we put our backs together and do what we had to do, but Shoap seemed to be a little more relaxed than me. We were basically against the whole club. We were on their ground, and they had the upper hand, so I thought. All of a sudden Shoap grab one of the guys and put a gun up to his head and told the rest of them that if they wanted to die, just keep coming. Shoap and I got a good distance away and he told the dude to run for his life and shot him in the ass. I didn't know Shoap was strapped; we were used to fisting to cuff, but I was sure glad that he had it. It was a close call, and I knew that they would probably give my description to the police and when they said from West Baltimore, I would be a suspect because the police knew who Blackface was, so I had to wait until the end of the summer, and I would start my new life.

The rest of the summer I spent most of it crossing the bridge with Junior. He had gotten himself a real nice girl. I knew her already, and we were really cool. So, when my uncle moved across the bridge, she would hook me up. I was a bad guy in a crowd of good girls. It was a lot of getting high and acting a fool. Of course, the guys who lived over on that side didn't like the way shit was going, but most of them heard about how I was carrying it and just a few of them would try me, and as I said, I was really good with my hands. By the last two weeks of the summer, everybody was over City Jail; my brother, Tim Black, Curley, Bob Shank, and Shoap were all on courtside. My man, Hank was a thinker. He started getting money with some dudes down Lexington Terrace and Whiz was doing his bid. It was just me, which was a problem. My mother was excited I was going to make it through the summer. It was the last week, and my girl; well, my main lady and my mother were close as mother and daughter. We all talked, and my mother told me to go and make something out of myself. My girl was ready to come when the time came, and my dad told me he had no doubt I was going to be alright. Uncle Esau and I just sat around and drank a couple of beers. The day finally came! It was September 25, 1980, and I was off to the

Reception Station. My recruiter was outside in a government car. I bet most of them thought something was going down illegally, but my mother and my girl were both crying. My girl was taking it hard. My best friend and next-door neighbor, Judy hugged me, and I was on my way to the United States Army Reception Station. I saw my man, Eugene, but that buddy wasn't working. We had a different path, so we would be going in different directions, but we talked for a few. It was a lot of sitting around and waiting to the point that some of the guys were changing their minds and walking out, but I had to go through it. I have always been one to finish what I started and how could I go back at this point. Not possible, so I sat it out. There were almost as many women goings in as men; I knew I couldn't punk out. It was never thought of because I was preparing myself for something different than what I was doing. After all, people who said I would be dead before I turned 16, and then changed it to the age of eighteen, were wrong. I had beat the odds! I heard Weathers and Weavers front and center I was already tight, but they were giving us a simple cut using one guard. I was cool with that, and we sat and waited some more. I started talking to Weavers, his name was Marshall and we were total opposites; one shade later, he would be white, and I was jet black but we were cool. He had a couple of joints he had kept. I didn't take a chance, but I helped him smoke and he told me he would hold me down if we ended up in the same unit. The rest of that day we completed our physicals and that's when it happens, right hand in the air, and we took the oath to protect our country. I was officially in the United States Armed Forces. The next morning, they loaded us on buses according to where we were doing basic training and Weaver went to Fort Jackson, South Carolina just like I did.

When we got off the bus, we were at an airfield and loaded onto the airplane. This was my first time flying and if this was how it was being on a plane, I would stay on the ground, but these were their planes and they got us to South Carolina in no time. There we had another period of waiting, but whenever it was time to do something, it always hurried up. It was followed by more waiting, and then we broke into squads and were given an M-16 rifle. The first day we were told that the M-16 was from this point moving forward for the next 8 weeks, our best friend. It would be all about combat ready and I mean ready. Every morning, before the sun comes up, we were up and at it. We did PT and started running our mile. It was cool because it was done as a team, so I guess that was the motivation. We had people barring up and the Drill Sergeant said, "from day one, everyone would not make it and he counted me out," because he knew where we all came from. So, he said, "The Baltimore and New York city slickers couldn't handle no pressure." He had the wrong one. That made me even more motivated, which I realized was his strategy; I excelled in basic. I was really having fun, but like every place else, somebody got to try you, so I had to beef with Ramos and Puerto Ricans from New York; their choice was either the army or jail.

Fuck him, we went at it, and he didn't have a knife and I would beat his ass. Afterward, we got sent to an adjustment unit, where after regular hours, we had special other shit to do in the Mess Hall. We had to clean the grease pit, which we had to do together. We both got tired of that shit and became cool, until one day about the second week Ramos came and said, "I knew your boys were soft in a bullshitting way." He told me, "To come to the barracks and give one of my homies some tissue and stop him from crying like a baby." I'll be damned if my man who I went to school with got there a week after me and was crying real tears. He was talking that go home shit. I had to talk to him, and he told me "You are a tough guy so this probably not hard for you because you been to jail and all," I wanted to slap the shit out of him, but I didn't. I told them to handle it like they were supposed to. See, the Drill Sergeant told us how they used to handle the "fuck ups" in the squad, and they would either shape up or ship out. The Army was no place for fucking crybabies, so we gave blank parties for people on each end of the blanket and a mother fucker couldn't move and you put fruit in a sock and beat the body, no face shots. We also would put a short sheet that was half made with all kinds of disgusting shit in the bed. The Sergeant was right and some left and some got tough. It was all good until the Sergeant got wind that I was making people shine my boots and shit. He called me out like a little punk from the hood. It was women around and I couldn't let him talk down to me. What I did but tell him the only thing that made him tough was just like the police their authority. I told this big muscle-bound Sergeant, "That I used to beat his kind," and the mother fucker told me, "After evening formation, he was going to see what I was made of." Boy, I stuck my foot in my mouth, but it was no backing down and sure enough, he came and got me, just me and he went into the woods. I must be honest; I didn't stand a chance. That was a fucking ranger, and he was built all solid, but I tried and each time he would have me on the ground. But I wouldn't give up; although I didn't have a win.

The next morning in the Pit formation he called me upfront and told me to keep up. I did, I got good; as I said, it was done as a platoon, so we were each other's motivation. It was nothing, we were running and marching ten miles and having field assignments.

Sergeant Duncan told me that he had taken a couple of people in the woods during his time as a Drill Sergeant, but I was the one who displayed some heart, and I kept trying and when it was over, I didn't tell the captain and he respected that. He kept the bar high for me, but I met every challenge. I was a good soldier in the making. I was an expert with my buddy the M16 and could tear it down and reassemble it in no time. Also, running codas right with him and he had a mean left flank. I liked basic, and I completed all the courses, but the gas chamber was my weakest point, and I still survived it. It was the last week before graduation, and I wanted my mother and my girl to come but chose to just wait, I would see them in a couple of weeks. Now we can hang out at the bowling alley or the beer hall. So, you know where you could find me. One night I was sneaking to the other side where the females slept, and I saw some of the Puerto Ricans coming across the fence and they were from Ramos crew. They were close too. I pulled Ramos up the next day and told him to tell his boys they better be careful because if I saw them, the roving guards might catch them. He said they had it under control when I asked what was going on. Those mother fuckers were cooping and shooting smack all along. So, you know I told Ramos to hook me up and he said, "They didn't waste shit going up nobody's nose." I laughed at him and when he saw how easy I could get on, he said, "so you been pumping all the time." I told him, a little about me, and he did the same. I didn't shoot up anymore that week, but I was going home for a week and then I'm on my way to Gordon, Georgia for my AIT training. I came home on a Delta flight, now this was flying a good experience. When I got home, Timmy was home and was happy to see me; also, like my mother. Then I knocked on Judy's door, we had always been really close. I kept on my dress greens and went towards Fayette Street for all the people who thought I was in jail. I could see the shock when they saw me in a uniform. I ran into a girl that was a real hustler and was in love with me. I would give her some time before I left again. Most of my time was spent with Bernadette and our son. I gave her my word that life was going to be good for us. She was finishing her last year of school and was going to AIT. Being home was really challenging and I was faced with several dilemmas, but I had changed. I only shot smack one time that week. Daddy had a smile of satisfaction on his face. Momma was bragging right now. She could say I knew Anky would be somebody and wasn't doing all the things that I was told. Little did momma know, but now how could I fail. I had to do this because all I ever wanted in life was to make my mother proud of me. Seem like this was the shortest week ever. I gave my main man, Tim Black, a couple of dollars. Nittnie and Poop were out back with the girl and a couple of others, so you know Poop was my ace. She told me that she misses me but she felt this was the best thing for me.

Poop and Curley was a big idol and he called me Gomer Pyle all in fun. Whiz was still locked up, and I ran into Shoap and he called me Sergeant Carter, still bullshit, but a step up from Gomer Pyle.

I sat and talked to my mother and father, then Bernadette was meeting me at Uncle Esau's house. He would always leave or go sit outside and Bernadette was no longer ashamed of being around Uncle Esau. It was just a respect thing. I was going to be leaving Monday morning, so we stayed Friday and Saturday. I wouldn't take Bernadette to the airport because I couldn't stand to see her crying again. I went home Sunday to pack my bags so bright and early I was at Friendship airport catching a flight to Georgia. When I got to the base, I was lost. There were no barracks, there was only a dorm, and I only had 2 roommates. The setting was one of a college and there were soldiers from every branch of the service, and I was going to be a 35 bravo, special tech support. This required a lot of math and too much math like trigonometry, algebra, and other stuff. All I knew were fractions, so instead of saying I didn't know, I started doing my high school strategies. I would get the girls to come over and help me, although I'm not going to lie, I could get it, but this jealous-hearted dude from New York would be my help. The girl he liked, liked me and he wanted to play Billy bad ass one night coming from the bowling alley. That was the hook-up spot, I was selling weed and the dude was jealous. So, one day he was in my dorm talking shit that I was failing in my class. Anyway, this was my chance, and I knew his punishment would be more than mine because he was in my dorm, so I hit him with an elbow, and it cut his eye. I was taken to the stock aid and was court marshaled. I was only an E2, so I went back to E1, lost 30 days' pay, and was kicked out Fort Gordon. That was cool, I still had a chance to straighten up because I knew my next move was dishonorable discharge. I was reclassified to another Mos which based on my entry scores, is where I should have been. I had a choice between a cook and field artillery. I chose to be in as a cannon crewman. I trained in Fort

Sill, Oklahoma. It was always hot as hell, but because I was still in AIT, there were barracks, but not quite like Fort Jackson, and was with some real hardcore soldiers. We did two jumps from the plane, and I was still sharp with PT, because I worked on the M109 Howizen big cannon or projectile were 90 to 110 pounds. We were taught how to use teamwork and as a cannon crewman, everyone in your crew was your responsibility. Then it happens, a friend and a fellow crewman told me to go in with him so we could check a gammon goat on whatever was available in the motor pool. I was looking at him and I could tell immediately that he was ill, the boy had a habit. I haven't even thought about any smack since my leave that one time at home, but when I saw what the people were selling for twenty-five dollars, dollar signs went in my head. These were huge for twenty-five dollars. It had to be bullshit, it had to be. There was the only way to find out. While he was trying to make sure I was cool, I was watching his moves and where was he getting his work and needles. It was a spot around the corner and several soldiers were doing the same thing. So, I just tried a little because I haven't pumped in a while. When I tell you it was some good shit, boy that shit was good, but I still didn't want to find myself in the military with no dope habit, so I would buy five and send them to Tim Black because by now he got a habit and had taken my spot in the street on steroid. He was a beast! He would always send me a hundred, but he could make at least a thousand. Fuck it, I didn't care anyway, that was my man, and I was eating and sleeping on post. I only sent money home, so my son, his mom, and my mother were good. I went on at Fort Sill and managed to stay low with my shit because I had some real serious obligations. It was time for me to man up and that is exactly what I did. I was focused even though my job was dangerous, and if it was a war, my job would be the first to be called. I was now a real soldier, so all the foolishness was in my rearview and things were going well. This was only a short assignment and once it was clear that we understood what our job was, we could get this coordinated and load the cannon. The training was complete, and we could be chosen, and two, to be tested on the time it would take to have the tank loaded and properly aimed. It was six (6) men to a team and the tank was all six (6) men's responsibility; any two at any time would be called to perform a task. Everything was done in twos, but never the same two. Everyone could do every job that was required to keep the tank operating, and I was good at each job function. During the week after about three (3) months of training, most of us were classified and sent to our permanent duty stations. I was told that my station would be a two-year assignment in Bamberg, Germany. I was allowed to go home for a week because my assignment was going to be after some of the guys who were already in Germany for two years were going home or I could just go to Germany and stay a week in the Transfon station. I figured I just went home 3 months ago, and it was hard leaving, so I just went on and took the twenty-three (23) hour flight to Germany. The holding station was in the downtown area not far from what is known as the Red-Light District. All of the soldiers who had come with me were warned about the danger of being in there. Marshall Weaver would be in my holding unit and his orders were the same as mine. Although it was suggested that we stayed out of the Red-Light District it wasn't off limits; so, you already know how that played out. Weaver and I had one hell of an experience that week. We managed to avoid getting arrested twice because the M.P.'s were cool. I got into one fight with a German pimp who felt I wanted to take his fucking spot. Our money was large once we converted it and we were playing the big shot. The real deal was the fact that we were street smart and recognized game. I would talk so much shit to these people and I knew when they were mad. They would start speaking in German and that's when it was time to fight or walk away.

Once I got drunk, I was ready for a good fight. One night I can remember it was that Thursday we were in a pub and one of the girls told us that some of the local dudes were planning to pull a surprise for me and Weavers. Their state, as they called us, represents the states and we were down for each other.

We were all either going to our duty stations the next day or catching a flight home on Saturday. None of that mattered, we had to be down for each other, so we were going to be pulling a surprise ambush on the locals. That night, I ran into a homie that was anybody from Baltimore, even if you never met, you were still home and he holds me in Germany to see any signs of weakness, especially in the 78th stallion, which was where I was headed. I told him what Tim Black told Momma, I told him not to worry because I am as strong as a box. He gave me some good pointers, but I saw it like any other situation, find the head, the ringleader. We were taught to kill, but I told him to pull back because he was going home, and he didn't need to get caught up in this shit. He told me that the MP's would be out with us taking care of this. He also told me that whenever the locals planned to plot on any soldier, it was all out of disrespect, and everyone was involved. He said, "that we were protected, and they should never plan any shit like what was being plotted no matter what." So, just as it was planned, it went down as a major brawl, and we came out on top. MPs didn't charge anybody and those who were arrested got handed over to the MP's. Weaver was stabbed in the arm, but nothing major. I had a stick and it landed on several skulls that were my introduction to Germany. That major! That Saturday came and we were all going in the direction we were heading. I was really happy for the guys that were going home because they were so happy. They said, "once they get back to America, they would kiss the ground." They were ready to go home after the shortest tour was two (2) years, and that's what mine was ordered to be. I would be in Germany for two years and it wasn't easy to call home, so I just adjusted to it with the mentality that this was the beginning of a new chapter in my life; after all, I had a family that I would be bringing with me as soon as I got back to the stateside assignment. I had already planned for the first time in a long time my life had a real purpose. I had something to look forward to. Before I left, I talked to daddy, and he told me that I could become whatever I wanted. He said, "He was proud of me." I talked to Uncle Esau, and he pretty much said the same. He said, "both of his boys will be in the service, you and Eugene." He also said, "he remembers when his twin went in the service." Uncle Elijah and so did Uncle George, my uncle who I stayed with in New York, we were all pretty close as a family. I talked to the boss, the one person who I moved the most and who I knew loved me beyond words and that was my mother. Mrs.

Ora is what everyone called her, but she was Momma and she set me down and replayed some of the things that people have said about me over the years. She said, "this was my chance to become somebody who would make a difference in life." She told me, "To set an example for my son and be a father like the one I have." Boy Momma raised the bar real high, but Daddy would be hard to compare. He was father amongst fathers, but I knew what she was saying. I saw a tear from Momma's eye, but it was different, she was giving me that look of discussion, but that was a tear of relief. She had one less thing to working about hearing the streets giving me a

death sentence. First, I would be dead before
I turned sixteen, and then I wouldn't make it to
the age of eighteen. But here I am, wearing
army fatigue, high school graduate, father of a
son, and heading off to another country in the
United States Air Force. Momma was proud of
me; that's all I ever wanted. Now I was in
Bamberg, Germany, and was good at my job.
All I was doing was drinking beer, well this had
to be the bean capital. The people refused to
drink regular water, because of the holocaust.
They believed that their water was still
poisonous, and the entire post was filtered. I
met my roomie; he was a smooth dude from
Haiti being in the service was a privilege for

him. He comes from poverty and was living the good life and loved to smoke weed and hashish. I would smoke but I was more into the music. You see my cousin was stationed in Fort Hood, Texas and we planned to get a club when we get out and it will be named Weather Pleasure Palace or Weather's Paradise. I was doing well and at this point, it was just a nine-to-five job. We had filed, exercised, and maybe guard duty, but other than that it was just like a job. After about my third month, we got a new gunnery sergeant, a big pure prejudice red neck. It was said that "he had a problem with blacks," but we would not allow him to get to us. We were at least eight percent colored and had our shit together as a unit. We did a great job at inspections and any two of us could perform our job duties without any problems, but this gunnery sergeant came in with a chip on his shoulder. He wanted to make something that was already meeting the standards to exceed the standard and I was jet black, so that was a problem. Our first sergeant was considered as being colored. Of course, we didn't want to have problems with this Gunnery sergeant, so we went along with his bullshit. First, we were addressing everyone that was in authority by the rank and last name, not him; he wanted us to call him Smoke. I just did my job and when he saw us working things out with ease the proper way or some reason, he felt that we could be better, and get more done if we stop teaming up, and did things that we were taught to do as two men teams. He just figured some of us shouldn't have help and I was the one he picked on the most. He would have me doing things that two people should do and the projectiles were heavy, but he felt for some reason I could do all this shit by myself. He pushed and I refused to let him beat me, but my corporal told me to report it and I did. I went to the first sergeant; I always followed the chain of command. My first stop would have been the sergeant, but we had a corporal and a spec forum, and they both came to me and told me that I should go to the first sergeant. I told him how I was being singled out and doing things that really should be done with help. The Gunnery sergeant was the corporal had words and before long, the corporal was reassigned to another unit and for me, shit got worse. I didn't call him Smoke one day so he had me repair a track on the tank by myself. This was most definitely no way I should be doing alone. All he kept saying was "figure it out because, in time of war, you got to figure things out." So, I went to the first sergeant again and nothing was done about this dude. We went on a field exercise and this dude locked me out of the tank during a Bore Hog invasion that was called in and the captain asked, "What was going on." But I didn't hear any more about it. It just didn't stop, I was experiencing hate from someone who was my superior, but I couldn't let this shit get me. I was being mistreated daily. One day during an exercise the track broke and his Gunnery sergeant Gunny is what he liked being called to me. To get a hundred-pound tunneling bar that was no problem, but again this was supposed to be a team effort and he had me doing it alone when I heard my back go out. I had sprung my back, my specialist told me to go and have my back checked out. It was bad, really painful, and I was put on light duty, but this fucking man, the Gunnery sergeant doesn't respect that, to him, it's just for little girls, so be disobeyed my restrictions, and I was ordered back to the ammo shed and told to stock the ammo. Now, these weighed between ninety to one hundred and twenty pounds, and I had to stack them. This is also something that we would do as a team. My back was burning and then my back started swelling up. I was rushed to the hospital and had to have immediate surgery for a hernia. I was in a hospital in another country. The Red Cross had contacted my mother and when I was able, they called and were able to talk to her. I told her, "I was ok," and then I explained how this all happened. She must have gotten in touch with someone because I really pissed this guy off. I had a light duty profile because the hernia almost caused permanent damage. I was really hurt, but I couldn't give up. I had people depending on me and didn't want this to be a cause. I was given some more examinations and was told that I would not be able to work as a cannon crew doing certain jobs, but I could still work on the field lines, and coordinate. I was already good in both positions. We had to know everything about those cannons, but this was not going to work for this Sergeant or Gunny. This guy just continues to torment me to a point that he said, "I was worthless as a man." I don't know what, but he would try to give me all the shitty jobs and try to violate my profile with strenuous work, but I just kept working and things were getting really personal with him. I told him, "He was the reason for me being in this position," and he said, "I was the kind of person he didn't like," and then told me, "I better hope we never went to war because I would be his first target." That bothered me because it was a fact that he hated me. We had another field exercise, and I was once again sitting on the cold ass tank. This time I got the piles; my hemorrhoids fell and that was just something I would have to deal with for the rest of my life, but not talked about, and it was something, The Sergeant would do shit and say shit like I am not worth a damn, and I was damaged goods. But I just pushed on taking shit from this guy every day, then we were called on standby. It was not an exercise; this was full combat ready. It was the Iran crisis. They had taken two hostages and we were in NATO in full combat gear and this mother fucker came up to me with his hand in the form of a gun with his two fingers pointed at me as if he was pointing a gun at me and blew the smoke from the barrel. This shit is really happening; any thoughts as I would be sent after by my tea and would have to get him first and then I remembered him saying, "He would never give me any real ammo." I was scared, but this wasn't the time to show it. We crossed paths and he did the same thing again so I had to do something and it had to be done fast. I thought about taking his pistol and shooting him right there then I thought about never making it home. So, I came up with a plan. I switched ammo belts with someone I could find. Whiz skills paid off. I crept in and changed ammo belts, now I knew I had real bullets. The second part of the plan would be carried out as soon as the balloon dropped the minute we went. Now there were some good and bad times while I was in Germany, especially when it was the weekend or after duty hours. My battalion was real crazy. It wasn't like in basic where if someone fucked up, they got a blanket party or short-sheeted. These guys were really inflicting pain. I saw four (4) guys put another dude in a wall locker and toss his ass from the third level of the barracks. I wasn't worried about none of that because I was no snitch. We did all types of shit on the weekends. On 2 occasions, I went to Amsterdam and when I say drug heaven, it was just that there was an open flea market type of setting, and all of the merchants were selling all types of drugs. This was the first and last time I saw pink and blue cocaine. They had liquid cocaine and black tar heroin. That was the first time I had ever smoked heroin, but I still preferred to shoot it. There were prostitutes and they were so pretty. Some of the guys went every weekend just to see a certain girl, but I only went for the highs, and when I would miss the train, I would be late for Monday formation and you know that fucking Gunnery sergeant would take advantage of the opportunity, but I didn't give a fuck. I was in the best shape of my life and still just nineteen (19) years old, so I could hang with the best of them. There were times when guys would be completely AWOL from the unit after going to Amsterdam which could be the result of an overdose on some of those high-powered drugs or some got caught trying to smuggle drugs back. Now I was told stories about guys who have been caught trying to smuggle drugs, who got an asshole lot of time in Amsterdam, and when, if they got released, they would be court marshalled and given more time with the Government, that wasn't worth it to me. I planned on having a future that would be successful and believe me, the dogs that they had on both sides were vicious, but they were trained to detect drugs and weapons. I went to a town called Wildflecken, Germany. Which was a town they considered an army town. There were war babies everywhere. These had to be some of the most beautiful girls I had ever seen, and they had been all about getting back to the United States. So, they were trying to get husbands what was said, "that most of their fathers were black soldiers," who had been left behind. Many guys were marrying those girls and they weren't fucking unless they were married. Shit, some of the guys, both black and white were the type that you could tell the most exciting thing that ever happened in their lives was happening now. I watch the guy get strip-searched at the train station and the dogs were on him so hard that they ended up finding a couple of ounces of raw heroin, so far up his ass it was in his stomach. Another time while on the weekend pass back down at the Red-Light District, I saw the pulizi, that police take an electric rod and stuck it straight up the German boy's ass, what a fucking shock. There were all types of shit going on in the different places. Now when I went to Newinberg, Germany, it was really to try and find my buddy, Sabby from the same block, the 300 block of Carey Street, and we did hook up and he took me to the wall. I had never seen anything like this, and even today as I travel all of the time, still never seen anything even close. This was the town for a good time and there I saw "The Wall." The Wall must have been at least 2 miles long and 4 stories high, with windows, and I swear each window there was a woman in it doing something to try and attract you. I swear this was the sex capital. Around the corner from the Wall was a park and there were naked women everywhere and they were selling sex. I can honestly say that for me it was exciting to see but nothing to get me aroused. I never spent money on sex directly. There was a Tavern that would be what we call a strip club, but sex was nothing to them, it was played out on television. The shows there if there were a sex scene, they had sex, no restrictions.

There was nothing left to the imagination and for me, it was a turn-off. Don't get me wrong, some women who had standards, especially in the town of Wildflecken, wanted husbands. Now, this was the first, last, and only time that I went to a nude beach. Everyone was naked, I was just a young man, and everything was in full working condition, and I was embarrassed when my shit got hard. I guess they could tell I wasn't a regular, but it was just something I experienced. Now don't get me wrong, they had condoms all over, but for me, it was not something that turned me on. Now the town where we did most of our field exercises was Grifinvilled, which was a real poverty-stricken town. That's where I got the plan to get my hustle on. See we had sea rations that we got from field exercises and of course we took plenty of weed and cigarettes with us because we would be in the field for two weeks at a time. That was also most of the bullshit I had to endure from the Gunnery sergeant. One cigarette was like a piece of gold to those locals in graft, and I told you till this day, German's don't drink their water, so I started selling the water purified. I sold so many waters purified every day I was going to the P.X., that's the store on the post and all you could get was two. I put the girl who worked down with me and we made a small fortune.

We paid maybe twenty dollars each, but they were selling for five (5) times as much, but it was marking that German money. Then we converted it back to American money. We were killing and then the cigarettes they had, but they were strong like stale tobacco and a carton of Newports was worth a small fortune. I guess it was worth it because we kept it going, but when I was recovering from my surgery, my partner had gone stateside, she has finished her town in Germany. I started working on my sound system and it was a real nice setup, and I had all the best shit. It was really cheap because a lot of the best shit was made overseas. I was getting better with things, and I had a good plan for the rest of my life. I got hurt at the hands of a prejudiced person, who in my opinion, should have never been allowed to be in control of people in another race. Things were cool for a minute, then I talked to my mother and told her that I didn't think the surgery was right because I still lumped my testicles. She told me, "To report it." And I did, but nothing was done. They said, "it was ok, and I just wanted to get back to work and work towards securing my future." But at that point moving forward my life would never be the same. Into combat, this would be the end of him, and I would get the ups on him before he would get me on my word. I would be the one to get him before he gets me. After about a week of this being on standby and me thinking about ways to pay him back for all the mean and hateful shit, he had done. The crisis was over, the hostages were released, and we were no longer on alert status. In a way, I was disappointed because I would still have to endure his bull shit every day. One day while attempting to do some light workouts, my back and hernia were hurting, so I just went and got some pain medication and was told that it would be to my advantage to take a medical discharge, but for me, that just wasn't an option. I had a life planned and people depending on me, so I went to the First

Sergeant for some advice.

THE DOUBLE CROSS

I consulted with my First Sergeant for some options and he said: "that he would look into it and see what my options were." I explained to him that this was my career, and I had a family to take care of. The first sergeant seemed to be willing to help, and I still got the same torment from the Gunnery sergeant; still vowing to kill me and how I wasn't shit, a fucking mess. This man made my life a living hell, but I would just not say a word to him because I felt it was what he wanted from me. I went back and I still had a lump on my testicle and my profile was extended, so the

First Sergeant told me, "That it was a medical situation, and I could take a medical discharge, or I could transfer to the mess unit, and change my MO's to a cook. I had a good friend who was cooking already, so I told the First Sergeant that I would like to stay in because I had plans, and this would be a big part of them. The First Sergeant told me, "That it would be a while, but he would make sure I get the transfer started," and I would soon be going to the cooking unit and would get the proper training from there and all. Although I still had to put up with the Gunnery sergeant's mistreatment, it wasn't so bad,

because now it was only a matter of time,

before I would be reclassified and would be

able to get my life back without being

tormented every day. This was where the

bullshit came from, and my life would never be

the same again. I was told that my transfer

had been accepted and that in one (1) week I

would be going to the cooking unit. I was

excited and told my mother who knew all about

some of the stuff I was going through, and we

both felt this would be a good thing and now I

could start to be more focused, and not have

to worry about being mistreated. I was in for

the shock that would ruin my life before it ever

got started. Somehow when I was called to sign my transfer, I was signing my discharge papers, and it wasn't even for my medical conditions. I was railroaded by the U. S. States Government. Now, what the hell was I supposed to do. I tried to find out what and how this could be happening to me, but I had no win. I guess my wrongdoings were catching up with my life and it was now a disaster. I just didn't have any idea what I would do, what could I say to my girl who had already made a sacrifice for me and the future. It was now all gone, and I was going to be going back home with nothing; no plan, no nothing. I was ashamed, hurt, lost, left with a hernia, and bad back, and an honorable discharge. I was screwed by the Government. In the beginning, I was isolated and all I could do to ease my pain was to self-medicate. I was out of control just using to stop hearing the Gunnery sergeant telling me, "I wasn't shit." I heard this for years. All the time my life was over, and it was because of him; was he right all along? Now at night, I had to still struggle with him, so I just self-medicated. My mother feels like I should contact somebody to help me with this because this was wrong; but Momma was sick, so I didn't want to bother her, and my girl felt like I held her back and she wanted nothing to do with me. I knew this was the same destructive way that I suffered and was trying to put behind me. But I just couldn't get this guy out of my head no matter how much I self-medicated, he was there. I started doing the things that I was doing, and I just didn't care. My life was ruined, and it was because of the fact that I was hurt doing what I promised to do for my country and at a young age. I used and abused and was lost, but I wanted to get this out of my head. It haunted me till this day how this guy said, "I wasn't going to amount to shit." I started drinking and right back using, shooting dope every day. I had to get rid of him, so I just didn't sleep because he showed up in my dreams. I had to support my drug addiction, so I returned back to the person I was trying to get away from, but only it got worse. I was having all types of close calls with the law and death. I was out of control and my mother was sick, so I did all I could do to keep my ways from her. I was stuck in the only thing I knew, I started dealing again, and Whiz and I got back together, and he got locked up and was sentenced to seven (7) years. I was burglarizing a warehouse with a friend, he got caught and I was in the ceiling about to get away and he hollered "come on and they got us. He snitched me out and I was over City Jail ill. I had a real bad habit. I was happy to get a toilet paper roll because I knew I was going to get on. I stayed for a week and at my bail review I got reckoned. I was back at it, I was in a shootout with some dudes in Franklin Square and I could use a weapon, but then I would hear my father say, "They only have to remember you." I had a bigger domain to deal with. The Sergeant was like a reckless fixture whenever I tried to change. He would be there in my dreams, so I didn't want to sleep, so I just did things to get into and use. There was a time that I robbed the big-time numbers man, and he had a contract out on me, so I went and got his son and made him call his father and I told him his son's life for my life. I never heard much from him, but I got a better idea kidnapping people for ransom, that didn't last long. I passed a couple letters to bank tellers, who I knew their family's movement. I studied these things because I didn't want to sleep and I needed money to stay up. I did the bank notes, but I saw a real close description of me on the television, so I abandoned that. Then I went down the projects and started robbing people and it didn't matter using or dealing, I just didn't want to have to see the Sergeant in my sleep, so I just didn't go to sleep. I was using a lot of cocaine with the heroin and always found myself in a real bad situation. Some guys that I robbed caught me slipping and I didn't have a gun and they were out to kill me, but I managed to get out by running in somebody's house and out the back way. The police were everywhere. I became paranoid and got my gun and that became a trademark. I had one thing at all times, a gun, so this time I got caught, but I threw it and the found it, but it wasn't in my possession and once gain I was on courtside. This time we were all over the jail on M-section. Tim Black, Shoap, Bob Shank and Curley. They had stores set up and all the jailhouse contraband. I had a habit and although they took care of me, I started going to the library to see who was and what was going on. One day at rec it came that it was going down in the yard; somebody I did something to was planning to set me up, but we were too strong, and I still don't know who this was or what I did. All I could hear was my father saying, "all they have to remember is you," you're the madness continuing, and how I have a big come up, so I was going to start dealing again just like a monkey selling bananas. I went to a good friend, and he told me straight up that he liked men and my brother had looked out for him and he would give me some product, but he knew we would become unbenefited because he knew I would fuck up and take his shit, and he will have to kill me or have me killed. He was a good dude. He gave me three (3) quarters; New York quarters; and told me from now on just bring him five hundred and he would look out for me. That never happened, he was found dead, set up by some of his close friends. I started going back and forth to New York getting back on top as much as I could, but I still had this dude haunting me, telling me "I ain't shit." I was trying to be strong when Uncle Esau died and that ripped a hole in my heart; first Johnny and now Uncle Esau. This just wasn't fair, and I couldn't process it so I backed off and start running. I got into so much shit that now my mother was telling me she feared for my life, so I took a break and got low. Nobody could find me until I got

locked up for an aggravated assault and

attempted murder. I knew it was Tim Black's

charge, but there was nothing in our DNA that

would say, snitch. I heard Tim Black saying he

would turn himself in because I was facing

twenty-five (25) years. I called him and told

him to chill, that would be snitching. My

mother had some bullshit lawyer at one of my

preliminary hearings. When I was being

escorted to the courtroom this stranger with a

black suit and a serious leather briefcase

came up to me and said, "You're Anky right?"

At this point what did I know to lose, I said,

"who wants to know?" And he said, "It's me

Jamie," And I said, "I don't know you." He said, "Yes you do. I'm the one you use to tell your boys to leave me alone, and you would walk me home." Then it came to me it was the one everybody called a coon because he wasn't like us, but now what was he up to. He told the Judge that I would have a new counsel and he would like a postponement. My mother recognized him and when I got back to the bullpen, he had them bring me to the Lawyer's booth and he told me that he would come to visit me in a couple of days, so he can go over my charge paper. Sure enough, he came in the next 2 days and told me to have 4 of my friends and Tim Black come to court and four (4) of them wear pea coats and a black beanie. I told him I didn't want Timmy involved because he did it. He said, "that was all the more reason" and to trust him. So, I got them to do what he asked and from what I was told, he had a victim to point to the person in the courtroom, who had assaulted him, and the guy picked one of the other dudes, he didn't even pick Tim Black. The attorney told the Judge that he would like for me to be released with all charges dropped because clearly, I couldn't have done anything to him because he swore that the person, he picked was the one who had assaulted him. When James came to the bullpen all he said to me was "it's over, you will be released, all charges dropped;" and he said thanks, but now we're even. When I got out everybody told me how cool this lawyer was and how he made the victim look stupid. I told them who he was and like them, we couldn't believe it was the same person. We all stood on the corner all the while he was going to law school, and he changed his bus pass for a little car and soon moved away. He had done well for himself, and we were all still trapped. I would keep doing the same old thing. This time when I got locked up, I was out on bail and Momma had her friend E.C. representing me. The 2 years turned into 2 years with the order to surrender me and start the 2 years before the end of the day. As we walked out of the courtroom after I got past the shock of being allowed to turn myself in, I looked at my mother and Mr. C., and they both said, "you're on your own, no bail or anything, just a warrant for my arrest would be issued at 2 o'clock." Momma gave me some money; Mr. C. shook my hand, and I was on the next thing smoking to New York City. I didn't go to my uncle's because I thought they might look for me. I was hanging out at Nostrand with Fonso, we were both young addicts. Fonso showed me a route to run from this government district, which was a good hustle, we snatch racks of furs or suits; whatever we could grab, and the catch was we sold them back to the person who was supposed to be getting the shipment. That only lasted for a while and things were getting kind of heavy in New York, so I went to New Jersey. My cousins lived in the Howard Street projects; hell, I was good, so shit as the Terrace or Murphy Homes I fit right in with the crew that was doing the dirt. Well for some reason I guess I was home sick and went back home. Now I am doing my thing and staying out of the way as much as I could and was living a dangerous life and I needed to get back on my feet. I went back to the stick-up game, where I caught a break and went and got a package from New York and shit was going well. I had Carlton Street wide open and even though I had a drug habit, I was doing okay. I got money and I was back to wearing the best shit. Little did I know I became a target some of the same dudes that I was pulling capons with had plotted on me. They knew I wouldn't be an easy target, so they violated the code, you see women and children were off limits, but in this set up I saw how those guys had sent one of the guys on their team to go and talk to my mother, my sister, my son, and some of my nieces and nephews on the steps. They had the ups and I told them they had me, so I went in the house and gave them half my stash and a couple of thousand dollars. We walked away together and my words to those 3 dudes were "all is fair in love and war." I told them, "That they violated me to the highest degree;" and they said, "it was the only way to get my attention, and they had no intentions to hurt my family." That was bullshit and now it was an all-out war, and, in this game, the odds were against them, because they put women and children in the equation, and I was hot. Later that week one of the guys was found on his knees shot execution style, someone beat me to the punch. He was the cruddiest of the three. A month later, I caught one of the biggest dealers in the project who he would later testify against, but I robbed the shit out of him, beat him with the gun, and made him strip, so he had to show up naked, and I told him, "All is fair in Love and War." The other dude got caught in a robbery and ended up going to jail and that got taken care of. Shit got hectic and I was back messing with my girl, who was a hustler. She was getting money and looking out for a nigga, but I was doing my thing. Momma would never take any money from me because it was bad money, so I would get a job just to get the uniform and I would wear it around my Momma, so on payday, she would take the money now. Momma knew that I was struggling with these nightmares about all the shit that the Gunnery sergeant had put me through. I couldn't get it out of my head and my hearing had gotten worse from all the times I was hearing the loud noises without him giving me ear plugs. This guy was still a major issue in my life, I just need him to leave me alone, so I kept using and when the high was gone, he reappeared, so I had to find ways to stay numb. I had to use something all the time just to keep from seeing this guy in my dreams. I didn't want to sleep because he was always there reminding me that he was right there saying, "I wasn't shit." I have nightmares about him killing me in NATO and no matter what goes wrong, it was always him with that nasty-looking smile on his face and the "I told you so."

For the next 6 years, I would struggle but then I started dealing coke and dope and working at the newly built Harbor Place, which was a condition of my probation; because the next time I would be arrested which would be another assault on a police officer this time. All of the people in the neighborhood were out and they told my mother about how the officer had started to conflict and were going to take me on a lot and beat the crap out of me. They drove my mother behind the cruiser to Western District, the Mount and Riggs station. The desk sergeant told the officer that he looked like he had a good ass whooping, and the police started talking a bunch of shit. I told him to take off his badge and gun, and whichever one of us comes out the back would be the right one, and I would not be charged. Well, he didn't go for it and without bail, I struggled over the jail because I couldn't get high like on the streets. I got high so I wasn't dope sick, but not enough to keep this sergeant out of my head. My ears are always ringing, and I don't know what this is. I finally go to court. The charge is thrown out and I had the escape from earlier, when I didn't show up to turn myself in for the two years, but the Judge told me, "Since you have not been in any trouble during that time and didn't cost the state," so he gave me time served, and I went home. Now I was once again in the park selling and using. My man Whiz came home, and you know I held him down, but he was the type he was all in or by himself, so I gave him some money and he went back to L.A. Things were going pretty well and one of my friend's girlfriends who knew I was getting money, turns me on to her sister. Well, in the beginning, it was for drugs, so I would give her drugs, but her sister was a cutie, and she wasn't into drugs just only smoked weed, but shit who didn't smoke a little weed back then. We got tight, and I had a way of testing girls to see how loyal they were. I gave the sister twenty-five hundred dollars ($2,500) and told her to hold this eighteen hundred ($1,800) for me. The next day I didn't go to see her, but she called me and told me that I had miscounted my money and she gave me the correct amount. Well, she was in, and she had a pretty baby girl, so I told her to take the seven hundred dollars ($700) for herself and buy the baby something. I invited her to my house, and she never left. My girl who was hustling came and she was calling me from the stairs. I told her to go, and I would catch her later; but before I got back to her, she was arrested and had gotten a bit after a couple of years of dating. I had gotten her pregnant, but although things were going well, and money wasn't a problem, I was still wrestling with the nightmares. This guy and the only person who I could confide in was Momma and she was tired and said, "she was going to speak to someone about the way I had been treated," we were going to when Momma got sick. I could tell Momma wasn't feeling well. Momma was a strong black woman, the best Mom, and friend. She was the best! Now I had a pretty little girl who was named Latia. Momma and Miss Doll Baby would always give me advice. This one-night Miss Doll Baby told me that I needed to get my shit together, because Momma's cancer had returned, and it was very aggressive. I didn't know what to do and the

Sergeant was blaming me for everything, and I needed the pain to go away. I would spend all my time doing the things to make my mother proud, and I could see what Mrs. Doll Baby was telling me. I had two little girls and one on the way and I always kept the girls close to me. So, this day Momma was in the yard, and she took Latia in her arms and told Carin to be a good girl. Momma told me, "No matter what happens, you have to be a man and take care of the girls, even the one that's not born yet.

SADDEST DAY OF MY LIFE

Momma had been taken to the hospital and was on life support. Daddy was a strong man, but his better half was leaving, and he wasn't ready for her to go. Daddy refused to pull the plug on Momma and Aunt Willie Mae told Daddy, "That she is gone." Now Daddy knew how close my mother and her sister and brother were; if Aunt Mae was telling him that he might have to make a decision. He knew that Momma and her sister were tight, both nurses and Momma was the oldest and at some point, she had to become the mother figure.

Momma never talked much about her family down south, besides Aunt Thelma and Aunt Maybell, who were her mother's sisters. That was the only family besides my aunt's children that we knew. Daddy told the doctors that he gives Aunt Willie Mae the authority to decide to cut the life machine off. I felt a pain that I never felt, my mother was no longer with me. My mother was put away very, very nice and the Church was packed. I was so high I wanted to be numb because I didn't know what to do. My addiction took off and I wanted somebody to just give me a reason, just any reason and I would surely kill them. I went crazy in the streets and couldn't hold down a job and I had three (3) daughters at the time, Meagan, Latia, and Carin. I was really in bad shape when Momma passed away. There was a big empty hole, and I just did not know what to do, so I did the thing that was the easiest for me to do, I went underground. I disappeared to make someone feel the pain that I was feeling and not the hernia or back pain from the staff I had been going through in the army. I really couldn't identify with shit and at this point, no one or nothing mattered. It didn't matter if I lived on not. I was pained and I didn't know how to stop the pain. I was so hurt to a point that I was using it all day every day. Word was that everyone was looking for me and I was hurt, and dangerous and it was just that many victims would come across my path. When I was in New York on a robbery capon, you see I had many friends in Brooklyn and Queens as well as Manhattan. I was just not a friend to anyone during this point and time. I was just out to try and fill the hole but the more I got the bigger the hole got and for that time I took so many types of changes that I should've been killed. I went on Nostard Avenue in Brooklyn, New York by myself and robbed the whole cee low game. That was the best dice game I could play. My cousin Lorenzo taught me at an early age, because "4,5, and 6 make your money grow rich,' but "1 deuce tray and your money went astray." At this time these were the same guys that I was buying from, and they always looked out for me, but fuck that, I want what they had, and I took it all. They started shooting and I expected them to because we would always have the banker control the bank and the money. So, I was a step ahead of them. I positioned myself up with the banker and the back way out of the shop but don't think for a minute that I was afraid and went home; oh no, I was back on Nostard Avenue not an hour later with stolen care and two pistols. I was high as Fat Charles' ass and my friend Fonze had got word that not only was I up there, but I had taken something from some supposedly dangerous dudes. But I knew I could trust Fonze, so I let him come with me. He was my age and he loved to get high. We were the only two in that crowd that was shooting smack at that time. He had a heart, but I didn't want him to catch hell when I left if I got away because I wasn't finished. I also had family in the Howard Street Projects in Newark New Jersey.

Fonze drove over and I know who had the shit over there and the plan was to take the spot off of me and Fonze. I didn't want to, but I ran into my cousin who lived in the projects, and he started telling me about some problem he was having with some dudes in his hood. I want to take care of that first and there was a big brawl. I went heads up with some weak ass niggas that were talking shit and asked, "what could you do without a gun." Fonze always kept that and crack the ole elbow to the chin and he wasn't talking anymore and now the dude who my cousin had the beef with, I called him out and he was a good friend of mine, but fuck it when worse comes to worst, the family must come first. There were some gunshots, so we scrambled and Fonze and I were in the building that my cousin lived in. There was a shooting gallery that I was very well known in, so they let me and Fonze hide out in there. We got high speedball all night, coke and dope together are a speedball up and down, back and forth, we were straight and good, but I was on a mission and I told Fonze to get ready we were going on the 7th floor, another spot, but this was the stash house. I was going to take it and that was my plan; no one was safe, and nothing was personal. I was really on a mission and didn't care about the outcome. I really been fucked up by the government and my mom was no longer here for me. What I wanted to do was to keep using, I wanted to stop hurting and maybe I would get my wish. We took the money and drugs and sat at the table and got high. By the time we made it to the car, we were ambushed by some weak ass project boys who didn't know we were not shooting blanks and we weren't talking. We shot our way out of that, and I could see that Fonze was getting tired, but he just didn't want to seem weak, so I let him off the hook. We went back to Brooklyn and to his girlfriend's house and I knew her and her sister from the tunnel. That is when the DJs took it to the streets and did their thing on the turn tables. We chilled and I asked Fonze, "did he want to come to Baltimore with me because I had some victims and spots we could hit," so he told me, "From this point you got the hometown crew," meaning I robbed New Yorkers that he know and he got the Baltimore niggas that I knew, Jersey and other boroughs we did them together. Shit was smooth, but so was my drug habit, it was out of control, and so I was caught up, that's all I did was hustle and get high. My cousin and I ran into some really good smack in Jersey. We both are greedy, and we slammed it. All I know is I could feel all the stabs and hits, but I just couldn't get out of it, and I will get all these mother fuckers who are beating me. My cousin Eugene was there, and he wasn't doing smack. He never did smack, but he was so fucked up about what was going on. I heard him say "nobody knows where he has been for about a month, and he show up and die on me." All he could think was about "What would Aunt Ora and Uncle Moses say about this," but I wasn't checking out just yet. Like I said, "I have had many overdoses because alcohol and smack just don't go together," and I love me some malt liquor. During those days where we partied in New Jersey at the club Zawzabar and the Hip Spot in New York was

Studio 54 and we had several in Baltimore, Odell's, Gasbys, and 32nd Street. My favorite was Club Capri on Thursdays, that's where the hustlers hooked up and showed off what they have, and I got a lot of my victims. I would tell Fonze to just wait and I pointed out the showoff of the night or who broke the crap game and had the loot. Fonze would get him, but on Thursday night shit went south and ended up in a big shootout, and I had to step in and help Fonze. Although he got shot anyway, I hit a couple because they weren't expecting me to come at them. I took Fonze to the hospital and they got him straight and he walked out with a limp with the bullet still in him. That made him even more dangerous, and he hates Baltimore dudes so that made it easier for me to put him on people. It wouldn't be a month later in New York when the same shit went down, I was shot in the calf and grazed in the shoulder, but I didn't go to any hospital, I was on the run. I took the bullet out myself and just got as high as a kite to stay numb. Coming up all we did was fight fist to cuff, but now, it was a different game, and I just didn't give a fuck. I think I wouldn't have cared one way or another, you know I felt like the government had fucked me over and made my life a living hell no one knew about. The night Mano's and the drill Sergeant haunted my life, so I didn't want to go to sleep because the shit that was happening to me at night while I was asleep was worse than my reality. I felt like the United States government owed me because they fucked my life up and now as a result I deal with deadly nightmares. I was wishing I could find a way to get back at the Sergeant for making my life a living hell hole. I knew I could and what was I supposed to tell people that I got chased every night and I was running for my life. So, I just did all I knew how, I ran away from all people I loved the most and turned to the streets and the game called survival "kill or be killed." My reputation was just that, in three (3) states, I was always on my guard and fighting for my life. I was

considered as Black who don't give a fuck and

I held up to other's expectations of me.

This went on until one day I got knocked off and the Judge only gave me the 3 years I had gone on the run for. In the beginning, suspended for all but six months, I went to the Penal Farm in Hagerstown, Maryland for 1 night and I was transferred back to Baltimore to the VOA because all I had was 3 months when I was sent up to Hagerstown. I was under the impression I had 3 years during intake. The mistake was caught in the city, I won't, I didn't mind, I was really tired and needed a break. Hell, the 3 years didn't faze me. But 6 months just helped me to come up with a better plan. I spent the New Year in Taconic, getting as high as I would if I was on the streets. I was thinking about a way out and my family that abandoned me and how I was treated. This was the entire government's fault, but I would have spent my life having those horrific nightmares, being chased by the demon. Sergeant, I was tired and didn't know what to do. I was now starting to feel like it was now or never; I had to give this shit up and start doing the right thing. I just kept thinking about Momma, "be a man, time to stop." I know what I told Momma was my reason and I promised Momma that I would take care of them, but now I was still lost and was doing so much shit in the streets that everyone was afraid that I was going to get killed. My sister suggested that I come to Ohio and live; well, we did move my family up there, but what that changed besides a different state, the same Anky. My sister had gotten me, and the children's mother jobs, and I quickly found the hang out because I had to find the happenings. However, everyone on the job was getting high. My sister took me to the store to get me some beer. They figured if I had a couple of 64 oz. bottles, I would be ok. As much as I loved myself some beer, it wasn't good without something else. I found the crowd and some of my sister's friends were the dealers in Ohio, so I fucken took their shit. They figured I did it, but they really didn't see me do it, and also that I was good with my hands. They plotted and waited for me to get twisted and they jumped me in my sister's house. What bothered me was she didn't help me, she let them jump me. I called Poop and told her what had happened, she told my father. When I went to work the next day, they gave me an ultimatum, either to go to treatment or be fired. I can't get fired because after being jumped I was about to take my family back to Baltimore. I took the 28-day treatment option, I had never heard about no treatment and this place was called Dartmouth and it was cool. I mean better than any camp or place I had been. The only thing was the dam meetings and group. I didn't mind going to those meetings at night called NA or AA; they were cool and a bunch of people drinking coffee and smoking. Most of them remembered me so I was good. I could get one of them to give me something, but they wouldn't, they told me to surrender to win. I thought they were crazy because when the cowboy or Indian surrendered, the other one was the winner. I caught on quickly and I started using my street smarts. I started using the language and I became a group leader. Meeting at 6:00, I was the person in charge, and the second week I took the community out for shopping and haircuts. That was my way in. I got a guy from my job to bring me some tools (needles), a bough-ready rock, a smack, and a beer back. I would stash it in the ceiling just like when I had my stashes at home. I saw the girl and two women exchanging pills, so I told them that they had to be cool and share with me and we would be okay. I got two other ladies, Dilaudid, she was smashing them. I already knew how to cold shake and shoot it and they were as good as smack. I let her have a set of tools for two dollars ($2). My roommate was a spoiled young white boy that loved to smoke ready rock. He would have people meet him at the meeting and bring his shit, but the rule was you had to make sure I got mine. This went on and everyone stayed until the twenty-eight (28) days were up. We all had to come for our completion ceremony and Jack, was a singer with the Ohio Player and a counselor, but it was Vernon who was my counselor. I told him that I fooled the hell out of the whole staff. Vernon looked at me and said, "the only person you fooled was yourself." "He still had his seven years clean." I just brushed that shit off and the whole thing was a joke. Take some cotton out your ear and put it in your mouth and surrender to win it was some bullshit. I went back to work, and I found where the petty cash was and I did one of Whiz moves. I kept them off and another dude got the blame. The next check day we would be going home. I got home and started my same shit over. It was one night that I had overdosed in the same park where I sold drugs, but nobody tried anything but called the paramedics. I would overdose a lot and I got tired of my kids seeing this side of me. I wasn't doing the best at keeping my word to take care of them. One night I was on my couch, I was feeling good, I nodded out and when I woke up the couch was on fire. I almost killed my family. It was time to quit, but I couldn't, so I ordered a couch from Rent a Center at a different address. All the furniture and TV came that way. I even made money off Ren A Center merchandise. Not long after I was home, my main man Whiz was given some bad shit because I had heard he beat a nigga that we knew and they set him up with a hot one, I never got to the bottom of the thing. Now I have decided to do my thing again because I had to keep my word and take care of my girls. Things were going a little better. I was looking out for my dad who was broken-hearted over my mother.

Two years later, Tim Black was using my sister's house as the stash and some of the same people who he was robbing and getting high came to try to rob them. They started shooting and Tim Black got hit, that was 1990, two years after Momma. Now Hank and I were out for blood that night. We were strapped and going to get them, but the dude was saying, "he never meant for that to go down and he didn't know it was my family involved," especially Tim Black because they were boys. Tim Black has a couple of friends that were straight killers, and word got out that they were also out for blood, so Slim turned himself in and got a twenty-five (25) year sentence. I couldn't process it, so I went on another binge. This time it was Bob Shank, and I went and got jobs down at the newly built harbor. We would wait until shit closed and go in the stores at night. I was in the bathroom and I heard the noise, Bob Shank had tried to hit the store without me and I saw them locking his ass up. I got the guy "T" a job. He was a good cook, and I was a prep cook, but we were at the biggest seafood restaurant down there. The hustler was sweet. I was in charge so I wouldn't account for a case of crab meat, shrimps, and lobster tails, and would get it by the dumpster and had my buddy come and pick it up. I was killing them, and they weren't missing shit. This went on for a while. I would send Bob Shank a cut and make sure he was good until I put "T" down with it. The hustler and I should have seen it coming because he started getting greedy. I had fences for the seafood, it was sweet, but wanted to take more, so I would take two instead of one and he could order more just by letting his supervisor know. I got my day off and had a plot with another dude that was working, and they had worked hard. They locked the guard into the freezer, pulled up a U-Haul truck, and cleaned the freezer out. The nigga that was with "T" got caught and tells everything, even what I was doing. So, they locked up "T" and the boy who was telling us. When I came to work as if nothing had happened, they locked me up, but they didn't have anything but somebody's word. They tried to connect me with the burglars that Bob Shank was charged with, but the picture was too blurred for them to say for sure it was me. I got fired and barred from this Harbor for life. Bob Shank got three (3) years and "T" got sixteen (16) years. Now, I was the only one from my crew because when I first came home Shoap and Bupor had a beef. I ran into him on my corner by the cute rate and Shoap had on a long trench coat, and I could tell he was up to something, and his problem was my problem, so I asked him, "What was up." He told me "He had a beef and he was going to handle it." So, I told him, "Fuck, we go together." When I started following him, he looked at me and said, "Man I'm not playing you just came back and you not going with me. I have to handle this by myself." He was very serious, so I gave him what he wanted and the next thing I knew, he was on the television screen for murder. My life has taken a turn for the absolute worse, but soldiers never give up, and now shit was as real as it gets. I was caught up and shit was starting to get out of hand. I was cruddy with a habit and not be trusted. I got knocked off in a raid, just so happened the weed house I was about to rob, was getting raided, so I threw my gun, and I was charged with just being there, but because of my record, I got eighteen (18) months. It didn't faze me, out of all the shit I had done, all my friends were going to jail, and I was trying to go, but now wasn't that time. I was sent on the transport to Hagerstown, and the very next morning I was called to go back to the city for VOA (Volunteer of America), because of the charge and my record I was sentenced to all but six (6) months suspended, so I was never supposed to be on the bus. I caught another break, 1990 came in and I was at the halfway house right across from the projects in East Baltimore. My cousin Eugene who was my right hand he would bring me some McDonald's, but the soda would be Remy Martin. I was on the kitchen staff and taking the trash out and realized that I could go, cop, some smack, and make it back and wasn't considered an escapee for the first thirty (30) minutes. I hooked up with my man who I knew from the streets, and we worked it out. I had the cup of liquor and went and got some smack, but I had no tools and wasn't a snorter, was always a shooter since day one so now what. We weren't the only ones getting high in the spot; the guy who was a guard was getting high and peeped him in a nod, so my man pulled him up and for a little bit on the hype, he gave us both a set of tools. My cousin would always make sure I had my shit, and I didn't want for anything. By this time, I was a little more stable and got out. My father was happy to see me because I told my cousin to tell him so he wouldn't be worried about me. Now my father wasn't doing well, to tell the truth. He pulled through stokes and hypertension but couldn't mead his broken heart. He was never the same after Momma left, but he was the strongest man I ever knew. I know that he would be ok, but I was told that he was in the hospital so I would go and see him. I had to go because I was back on the streets and my addiction was back in full force. One day my sister Netta told me that my father wanted me to come down to the hospital. She only had to tell me once. No matter how hard shit got, I knew who my priorities were. Now I was feeling good when I got down to the hospital, but daddy was different and must be talking out of his head. Daddy just as plain as anything said "Anky, go and get the suit that you brought me and get it cleaned so I can wear it when I go see my father." I said, "daddy, your father is dead, how are you going to see him."

My father said with his authority, "Anky, have my suit cleaned. I want to wear it when I go see my father." I'll be damned if my father didn't pass away later that day. Meanwhile, I had his suit cleaned as he asked me to. Daddy was structured, he always laid down his law and would often take me to the cemetery where Momma was and showed me that he expected me to keep their grave sites clean. Now I was what you might call, "my street rap was dying" and my concussion was awakening, and I started drinking more than I was doing anything. I still had to drown out the Gunnery Sergeant; he was now as loud as he was in the beginning. I can't stop the nightmares, he wants to kill me, and it seems like he wants to use me to do it. I'm struggling and now life is starting to take a real toll on me. I'm starting to rob people's stash spots and now and then somebody would just give me something because they feared I would take it. Until one night I was on the pried and ran into some guy from Calhoun Street Bridge. One dude said, "Man, give Black something so he doesn't have to worry and owe me." The kids said, "Fuck Black, he isn't getting shit, and nobody scared of any old ass nigga."

I snatched his shit he had about twenty (2)

bags and about twenty (20) niggas jumped my

ass, but I held one of the kids in front of me

and I never let go of the drugs. That was a

good night, but my pride was fucked up and I

didn't get hurt when I got jumped. I went and

traded some dope for some coke and went

and got good and high, then I grabbed my gun

and went back and shot in the crowd, and on

the way back home I ended up selling my gun.

Now I don't know what the hell I was thinking

about but that was my line of defense, I sold

my gun and from that point moving forward my

life went all the way downhill. I reduced myself

to a bum and was too ashy to go around

people I knew. Then I saw my neighbor and sister Judy. No matter what, she never negatively looked at me and Judy said, "Anky you need to get yourself together, your mother would not be happy." I knew that she was right. Now at this time, daddy had been gone for a year, and when I tell you I was a bum and was on the run from taking somebody shit. Poop always had a place to stay and no matter what, she took care of her children as she was told. I'm sure because Momma told us all she did her best for her children, and we have to do the same thing for our children. At this point, I wasn't doing much for myself but what woke me up was one night I was hiding and went to Poop's house. By now she and my brother, Tyrone is getting high and were downstairs where they had some dope and coke. These were my siblings, so I went down, and they both had a good bit and when I asked them for some just to get the ills, they denied me. Now not Poop, Tyrone I could see, but when my ace watched me be as fucked up as I was, and she wouldn't give me anything. I was so hurt that I said, "Fuck it, I'm not hiding if something happened to me, she would feel bad." When she saw me trying to get straight to get out, she had the nerve to tell me to go lay down. I told her "I was ok." I walked to the three hundred 300 block of

Carey Street and my mother's friend who had her children would always look out for me and she was sitting by her window and saw me, called, and gave me ten dollars ($10), which was enough for a six-dollar ($6) dope and three-dollar ($3) coke. I split it up and made sure I had enough to get started. The next day I went to the tree, to the cut-rate, and had a gate partner. We would make it happen every day somehow and then back under the tree drinking wines, night train, and conakka, the worst drink I ever tasted in my life. It was just one dollar and thirty-two cents ($1.32) for a pint. I would gulp half down. It wasn't something that you wanted to repeat. I called

Eugene BKA Box, he was back in New Jersey, and he was doing well for himself. He was still my ace, and we were really tight. Box reminded me that we were both blessed, and he had given up to live life as a man should. We talked about old times and how Wiz could still be in jail for interstate trafficking. We had gone to New York in Brooklyn and bought ten (10) bundles of coke, ounces of powered cope ounce of rock, and some weed. We got stopped four (4) times from the time we left Brooklyn, in New Jersey, New York, Delaware, and the last time while still on the New Jersey turnpike near Philly exit, we got stopped. They searched the car and started looking at porn magazines. They were calling for the dogs, I told Box, "I was going to run." But he said, "chill." I stood up, and the police told me, "To sit back down" and then they got a call for all units. The cars that were coming with the dogs turned around. They gave Box his keys back, I jumped in the back seat and when I woke up, we were on Saratoga Street in front of Netta's house. As soon as Box opened the trunk, all the drugs hit the ground. I told Box that I was proud of him for doing what he was doing but the truth was I felt abandoned all by myself. Shoap had come home and gone back for shooting at this police. It was just me and I was a fucking bum, a bum with a conscious. I started going around my children more often, they were preschoolers. I would attend, but I smelled like alcohol. Miss Sye was there, a real good friend of my mother's and she pulled me up and gave it to me raw. She straight told me, "I was better than what she was seeing, and my mother would turn over in her grave." That hurt, but that was true.

Momma

When I say those words, I say them with all the existence of my very being. I was one of the fortunate ones. I had Mrs. Ora Weathers to call Momma. She was a beautiful black full-figured woman and the most loving and caring person anyone would ever meet. My siblings and I had the pleasure of calling her Momma. Momma had eight (8) children: Ruth, we called the oldest sister; Maythelma, who was named after Momma's two sisters, Aunt Maybelle and Aunt Thelma, who was also the only relative I would ever meet from that side of the family; Johnny, who was named after his father, that's where he got his style and street smart from, that's what I heard, but he always told me that in this world you have to be the best person you can be and he was just that and had a million dollar dream that ultimately cost him his life at an early age; and then it was us, the eight (8) children who had the most loving and caring parents in the world. Momma must have made it her life promise that she would be the best mother ever and succeeded with just being that. In our house, there was Moses, Jr. Tyrone Moses is what they called him. He was the big brother that would always be there, was a jack of all trades, and was the best at whatever he did and that really set the bar high for us. In baseball he would be the first picked player in all the leagues and played every position on the field, in football he was either wide receiver or quarterback, and give him a bike and he would tackle dead man's curve, believe me, a many have met an ambulance at the bottom of the curve, ball bearing, #skates and kept spare wheels because he could skate, carpenter, mechanic, master electrician, and a real ladies man and also in the Air National Guard. He was a later bloomer in the drug game but became the best at that which tied him to an all-time low. He became someone he didn't know in his ending day; we talked, and I got a chance to tell him that he was once the person most people would dream of being. Tyrone died and it was like Johnny was a direct result of the lifestyle but had body organ failures. He had some beautiful children that now call me "Unc." There was Cynthia, BKA Nittnie, who was a beautiful red-headed freckled face girl and was very well loved. When we were little, she would always tell me shit like you like to start a bunch of shit and I would always aggravate her, she could really throw down fighting, was not something she would start but she would whip the average girl up to five years older ass with ease. At one point,

Nittnie and I had a love hate relationship and it was personal and nobody else can get in our drama. She would call me a big black liver lip bitch and I would call her a red freckly face orphan, most of it was just sibling drama, but we knew we had each other's back. In later years she watched out for me the most when I was homeless a couple of times, she would toss me her keys to drive her car because she knew I could drive because she knew I was stealing cars. Now she was really a late bloomer and got caught up on that ready rock. She became one of the best cooks in West Baltimore, which made her addiction really take off and we both became homeless. In our parent's house, good old 318 Nittnie finally got herself together to be a part of her grandchildren's lives and did a great job of it. By this time, she was always telling me how proud she was of me because I had become the man that God intended for me, and my parents raised me to be. We both were Harry Potter fans so when I went to Disneyland, I bought her a wand back. She told me she wanted to go to see Hogwarts and I had the privilege of taking her to Disneyland. She had a ball. I told her bout New Orleans; she was planning to go with me next year because she wanted to go to Mother's Restaurant and eat some crawfish. Well, although I have made

New Orleans one of me go places, I haven't yet gone to Mother's Restaurant, but by the time you read this, I will have eaten there. I love me some crawfish. My sister and I really miss her at the card table she could play spades and loved the game. She would invite herself and some friends to my house and we would play spades, they would have their spirits, but she would make sure no one even thought about offering me anything. Nittnie often told me how proud she was of the way I had changed my life. She heard those people saying I would be dead before I turned sixteen (16).

My sister went on a cruise, she told me she really wanted to go, and I helped her, but she was never well after that. She really got sick to the point that she couldn't move her limbs from the neck down and was put into a Nursing Home. She could talk but was very limited, and I went there every day. We made sure they knew she had people who cared. She once again gave me the car keys although I had my car. Nittnie went to heaven to be with the rest of those God-called. The neighborhood really showed up for her and I was extremely happy to see just how much she was loved. Then there was Delores Loving, known as Poop. As kids, Poop,

Timmy, and I were three (3) the hard way.

She could beat most of our friends. Poop was

a spitting image of Momma, was dark

complexion and one pretty black girl, but was a

bad ass and smart as a whip. Poop was

always on the honor roll and wanted to be like

Momma, so she went and got her Nursing

Degree. Poop always did for herself and until

this day she is my ace. Poop had her part with

the disease of addiction, but never did shit to

disgrace herself because she and her

childhood sweetheart had no need. She and

Curley met at Harlem Park and out of all the

guys chasing her, Curley was her choice. He

was a straight-up hustler, then a big-time drug

dealer, so the shit was at her dispense, but don't get me wrong, it was her friends that got her started not Curley. Although he would give her anything, she wanted to be in the streets when Curley got locked up. She always kept her family together and her two (2) children always had the things that they needed. Poop later came to me and told me that she had had enough by this time I was an Addiction Counselor, even to this day. Poop had seen me and my friend Zaid who started Recovery in the Community, she told me, "She was tired and wanted to get clean." All I would say was "thank you, God." Poop did what she was told and never looked back. I'm sure she has at least twenty (20) years clean. We both were and still are a part of the fellowship of Narcotics Anonymous. Poop has a special calling; she is now an Evangelist and studying to become a Minister. I could not be prouder of Poop. She has a beautiful spirit and does the work for God with all of her heart. Poop took her skills and started her own business as a Care Provider for the Elderly with Independent Living. She is very dedicated, my go-to person, loves the Lord and if you come in contact with her, you will feel the Grace all around her. Today, she is my big sister and helps me to keep my head on straight and I love her to life. Then there was Timothy, well of course me right behind Poop, but there was Timothy, AKA Tim Black. Timmy from day one was my shadow, was just a year younger than me, but for the most, if you saw me, you saw Timmy. I remembered as little, tiny boppers; we made a pack that we would always look out for each other. Now Timmy was very cunning, and he liked to let me go out front and he defiantly had my back. As I sit here, just the thought of the childhood I had with him, makes me sadly happy. All Timmy wanted was to do him. He stayed in some type of bullshit even when we were little, like Tyrone. Timmy was nice with his hands and also could play all the sports. Timmy got his own identity when I went into the service. He had his shop selling

coke and dope, but before then Timmy loved

to fight and had a one-and-done punch. He

started hustling and would do anything. The

entire real street hustler wanted him to ride

with them because, like me, he was loyal and

wouldn't leave you. He was in 161 when he

first got into stealing. He and Willie, our God

brother were thick as thieves and two little

dudes raised so much hell. Timmy was the

favorite and daddy told him to start taking care

of himself, because if he had your back, he

had yours, and believe me, he was true to the

game. Timmy became an enforcer at an early

age. His weapon of choice, his hands, see

this was before guns were popular, but eventually got his hands on a gun and that became his trademark. See I got into drugs, and I swear I did everything I could to keep it away from Tim Black now, but he got on and he went off and started doing the things I was doing. Although it seemed like he got worse and the whole neighborhood was afraid of him. We were selling drugs and he would still take the shit we sold from the people. Timmy got to the point that he was off the hook. My dad also told us that it is not smart to have everyone afraid of you because you would have no allies. We never listened to Daddy anyway, but we got into shit. Timmy went to jail on several occasions and told my mother the first time he got a sentence his words to my mother, a good Mom, stronger than boxed lye. He lived up to that because he was the same way in jail, was just so good with his hands that most people feared him, and quickly became his friend. I watched my baby brother go down and we would either have our own or he would hook up with a friend. Timmy had our sister let him use her house as the trap house and on this day, another local stick-up kid, one who he had done capons with, came to rob the stash house as it was his position. He tried to avoid the stickup and did but he was shot in the process. This was a set-up murder. We looked for them for a couple of days, but the police got to them first. Timmy died as a direct result like my other two (2) brothers, but they will always live in my heart. Now we got to the baby of the bunch and that is Runette, BKA Netta, she was always everybody's favorite and knew it but just like the rest of us, she could throw down. Netta was always the one to hold everything together. We never had a time when struggled over who was the favorite because we all were loved, but Netta was protected by the rest of us. She has the same type of nurturing spirit as our mother and at one time or another, we all went to Netta for this or that. She was very spoiled, but she had a short temper. If you don't want to hear the truth, don't talk to her. Just like my mother, she became the go-to person for all the children in the neighborhood. I swear they are all grown, but they still love Miss Netta. She helped raise all of our children and did a great job at it. Now Netta and I still have a great bond and she always tells me that she is proud of me. We maintained a special relationship when I was down. I wasn't out because I could depend on her, and we are still like that today. Now I told you it was always eight and that is Brian, my brother's nephew Momma got Brian at probably age three and he lived with us. We never even thought about anything but brother

Brian. He was really quiet when we were

coming up. But he could look at something

and draw it as he saw it. He lived in the same

house, so it was the same rules. He was a

South Paw and was sneaky, but nobody

fucked with him. Brian was more of a ladies'

man and came out of school and started

cooking. Now he is the Head Chef for two

restaurants and all through his addiction, he

worked but had a couple of "hiccups" and did

his time for his hustle which was based on

making money. Heard more than seen; today

he is doing well, has been clean for about ten

years, and now has a new home and a

beautiful wife. Then there's Ronnice, BKA Princess. Coming up Princess had to come into her princess was a real pretty redbone, so she had her little ways and was very manipulative. I was shocked when I found out that she was a good hustler and was just like the rest of us. She had to find her way to she and her little chick were downtown taking shit. She was very popular in school and grounded, but soon got her hands on some crack and so went all that innocence. She finally followed me and Poop into the fellowship and put some time together and relapsed but thank God she didn't lay down. She got back up and how to have thirteen years clean. She recently lost her husband but stayed on the bean. Princess loves social media so you can friend her and meet her for yourself. You see why I tell you I was blessed because there was a lot of love in our home. We all have children and see what it must have been like for our parents. Now like I said, Momma was diagnosed with breast cancer, and we all went through a rough time, but Momma had her breast removed and faith in God never waved, she pushed on. She must have asked God, "to allow her to make sure that her children were alright." He took her home because she didn't want the chemo or radiation. She fought that thing and I swear to you she made sure that we all had our own homes and at least tried to do our best. We all had houses, and vehicles, and my second born was the last grandchild that she would hold. Momma told me that day that the unborn baby would be another girl and told me to straighten up my life and take care of those girls. Momma passed away and Heaven opened to receive one of God's most precious angels. It took a minute, but I eventually did my very best to make my mother proud because all I ever wanted in life was to make my parents proud of me. I know Momma is in Heaven, but she also lives forever in my heart. But Momma had a forever partner.

DADDY

Daddy was a proud man. He is from the South and was raised with his five brothers and sisters. My father was a man's man to this day. I wish I could say that I am half the man that I saw in my father. Daddy was wise and very seldom did you hear him. But when he spoke you better believe we heard him. Daddy was a hard-working man who loved his wife. I mean he adored Momma and was 100 percent a provider. I can honestly say that

Daddy made sure that we wanted for nothing. We always had everything we needed, but we were fortunate enough to have just about all that we wanted now. Daddy came from Sumpter, South Carolina, and his first job was with Oline Chemical Company and that was the job he would work for his whole thirty-five (35) years. The owner of the company sold Oline to another company and Daddy had twenty years, but they told them that Daddy was part of the deal if he didn't keep everything that he had vested, they would not sell the company and the owner of the new company loved Daddy as well. He was a hard worker with a good work ethic. Daddy would often take us to the airport, and he got a kick out of watching us go at it until he stops, and anything pass one stop and he joined the party and didn't like that. Daddy was a real disciplinarian, meaning he whooped our asses with whatever he chose as a weapon. Mostly it was that size 54 black real leather belt. When he pulled it from around his waist it went straight to the target. I got plenty of those but today I am grateful for each lesson. My uncles often told me stories about when they were children and how my dad was a big bully. They say he was tough, and nobody fucked with Moses' family; kind of sound like his son, but now he was instilling lessons in us that I didn't get until I was thirty-four (34) years old.

After all my insanity, all I live by now are the

things that he instilled in me years ago. Daddy

loved wrestling; that was his pastime. I could

remember a couple of times when we were

young, he would go to Cherman's Bar down

the street and his dog Frisky would be right

outside waiting, and he would have words.

They would run to get my mother because she

was the only person to calm him down. Well,

his aunt Tang could but she was in South

Baltimore, so Momma would just call his name

and that was it. I heard some words between

them, but he was too much of a man to raise

his hands at her and never cursed at her.

That's why he told me once that I was an insecure dude, and he didn't know where I got my cowardly way when he heard I was hitting my girlfriends. He told me, "I needed someone that no one else wanted and I would stop acting that way." I remember the time my father had heard me and Timmy in the room and we were laughing about the fact that I was taking a lot of different drugs all on the same day, also how Timmy heard that I was robbing people like I was losing my mind. Timmy was asking, "What was going on," because this was unusual for my father, but he feared for my life. My father told me two things, "First, he didn't know why I hated myself because anybody that would do that many drugs are trying to kill themselves, and secondly, going around causing harm to so many people would also get me killed because you could never remember all the people you cause harm, but all they had to remember was one person, and that was me." All that meant nothing because it wasn't long before it came true. I almost got killed and to this day I don't know who was shooting at me. Daddy was one good role model. He led by example and what I saw was a man that loved his family and adored his wife. I could never be the man that Daddy was, but I am going to keep trying. Daddy had a couple of strokes; once outside the Civic

Center and the paramedics tried to get him to go to the hospital, but Bobo Prozil and Chief J. Strongbow were going to be wrestling. Daddy got himself together and went to watch the wrestling match. The only way Mom knew they had called her when it happened, so when she saw Daddy, he was getting ready to go to work. He was the best Daddy in the world, and he will live forever in my heart. I watched Daddy go down as a result of a broken heart. Daddy was strong as boxed lye. He carries the torch like Momma would have wanted. It was just four years later that Daddy had another stroke or something. All I know is Daddy had talked to God because he sent for me to come to the hospital to see him and told me, "To get his suit ready because he was going to see his father." At that time, I was not aware that he meant God. So, I said, "Daddy your father is dead, and you can't see him." He told me what he wanted to be buried in because he would never come home from the hospital. Daddy left now, I really changed, but I didn't realize it. Daddy also showed me what he wanted from me because he would always take me with him to clean up Momma's gravesite, so that is something that I take pride in doing. I also know that my parents are with me because I am living in the truth today.

UNCLE ESAU

Wow, when I think of my right-hand man, Uncle Esau. Well, I called him Joe and he called me Joe all my life from a very young age. After the fire, Uncle Esau came to stay with Daddy; they were as close as any brother you would ever meet. He had six (6) brothers, Uncles William, Moses (my dad), George, Esau, and Elijah (they were twins), and then Uncle Nieamione, all names from the bible. In my lifetime, I would form a personal relationship with all my uncles, and they knew about the relationship that I had with Joe. I was just learning the shoeshine and I watched Uncle as smooth as ice, another hard worker; I guess that was instilled in them as they were growing up. I was a talker and I had started by bull shit game and Joe got a kick out of watching me make my moves. In the beginning, I would always tell the ladies that Joe was watching. They would put on a show for him switching and flirting then Joe would make his move then would come home. Joe and I would talk about the truth, whereas he missed his own family and his youngest was my age and his daughter was the apple of his eye. He would always tell me you will see him and one day y'all going to be close. He was wise and was right, but Joe would take me damn near everywhere with him. A lot of the times he was helping me to get away and I would go to the projects or somewhere and do whatever. One day I was with Joe with his wagon and Joe didn't bother with them, but he really got a kick out of watching me put them away. Listen, I want to say that everyone should be so lucky to have had an Uncle Esau, no matter what I knew, I could depend on my man Joe. Although he was getting word about the things that I would eventually start getting into. Joe never once turned his back on me. Don't get me wrong, he always told me that I was wrong when I was wrong. He reminds me that my parents or he didn't raise me in the way that I was going. Also, he said that as a young man we will make some bad decisions; all he asked was that I didn't keep making the same ones. There were times when Joe would just say come on and I had no clue where we would be going, and it didn't matter. He was making every effort to help me change, but he will always have a girlfriend with a daughter, and little did he know most of those girls were on syrup or something. So that's cool, I would get two for one eventually, just like Joe told me. I would meet his son, my brother from another mother, Vincent, Eugene, or Box, all the same, and me and him were thick as thieves from day one, and Uncle Esau never switched up on me. He looked out for both of us and in some ways that was a great help because I couldn't involve Eugene in the shit I was doing, but believe me, the boy was far from being grown. Uncle Esau was really tight and I knew that his guidance was a big part of the fact that I survived the streets with all the different lifestyles, choices, and decisions. I had a place to go, 534 Carrollton Avenue and that was a hot block basically a bunch of beautiful young girls who had mothers in the beginning. I was the new kid on the block and all the women were on Joe, so they weren't paying attention to the fact that

I was making my move and I had two (2) really close female friends on the block. It was all just something to do until one day my mother told me and Eugene to come with her and we went to the hospital where Uncle Esau was working, and they told us he was dead. What are those people losing their fucking minds, Joe was just fine last night, what the hell are they saying? It was true, another dark day in my young life and I couldn't process it now; there were two of my idols gone. But if you have been fortunate enough to have a dad and an Uncle Esau, then you know what I am saying.

GUNNERY SERGEANT

I have been in a lot of things in my life, but nothing had had the effect that I experience with this Gunnery Sergeant. When I first got hoodwinked and my life went downhill from the fact that I was put out of the service wrongfully. For the next forty years of my life, I would experience the drama night after night. I was

medicating myself because I didn't want to have to experience what I had to endure each night. Until this very day, imagine yourself in a place that has no meaning in every way you go.

There is another challenge and you're defeated by the same demon, but so many different scenarios. I find myself on a battlefield having to run for my life because there are several of this same man carrying me and I have no defense but to hope I wake, and it is a dream. How about being in a house with a thousand different doors and behind each door is something waiting to cause you harm and the bottom falls and you go down. This Sergeant demon is just laughing at you, telling you were never worth a dime or find yourself in a nightmare or where he is the judge and the jury, and you are sentenced to a punishment of lifelong torture. That is just some of the shit I experience nightly for the past forty (40) years of my life. I was finally getting help with Mrs. Debra Foster, the sweetest lady that I met after my mother was no longer with me. I started doing something that I didn't think I would even be capable of doing again and that was to trust somebody after the way I was treated. I had a vigil heart, but I found myself getting in a very caring and trusting relationship with Mrs. Foster. I told her what had happened to me and the fact that I was young, and Mother got sick before I could get some help with what the cause of my life was going back to the ground. I got honest and told her about some of the things that I did as a young man before going into the Army. I thought this is maybe payback for my action and she said, "No, you were taken advantage of, and it was some racism involved." She told me, "I should file a complaint" and she was documenting our session. I loved Mrs. Foster and she started helping me and I could see her twice a month. I was now drug-free so I had nothing to help with the nightmares, so I was given medication for PTSD, Depression, and Anxiety, but nothing would stop him. He was everywhere. I started taking medications to help with my sleep and my back pain which was at a level ten (10). The VA used me again and they gave everything you can think of for my back and that included electric shock treatment. The hernia would reappear about three (3) more times, and I would have to have surgery; but no matter what I did, until this day, I can't get rid of the trauma that I suffer as a result of my volunteering to protect my country. I still feel the injustice every day, wrongful relationships and a year of constant pain, and the night trauma of the nightmares of being sent after and having to defend myself. As I got more involved with the NA Fellowship and became more established doing work on myself daily, things in my life were starting to get better. I watched Mrs. Foster just as I watched my mother, they fought until it was just no more fight in them. Mrs. Foster passed away, but she made me promise to never give up. I am still in the fight right now. I suffer from great body pain and because I refuse to be looked at in the worse way, I don't communicate with my PCP because she only sees things one way. I have nightly nightmares and the fact that I fear to sleep now. It happens during the days I'm battling the demon. He wants my life, so I just pray because I know that I have survived a lot. I did a lot, but I don't have a punishing God, so it's just something that hasn't been figured out yet, but I won't give up. The first thing can be very hard at times, but I got a second chance at life, and this was bought from the old life. Well,

that has been the struggle, the old demon

Gunnery Sergeant wants me to believe that "I

am not shit" and "won't amount to shit." Some

of the people from my past said, "Things

similar, they even gave me a couple of

expiration dates," boy, I'm glad they weren't

God who is the real Judge and jury. Over my

life has had meaning and just like my personal

angel, the one sent to guide me to a new way

of living saw the purpose and told me to help

someone just like she helped me. I have told

the story about my angel and the fact that no

one knew who I was talking about and have

seen the looks on people's faces, the look of

disbelief. It had to be someone to help because of myself I would have been self-destructed, but instead, I was afforded a whole new life free from everything, but the demon Sergeant. I have been clean and serene for twenty-seven (27) years and every day of the journey I have done my best to help someone and become the man that I am proud of being. God had taken this mess and made it a message. I have been haunted for the past forty-plus (40+) years and have had several life changes. I've been a very blessed man who has been afforded a second chance at life and when I tell you that I can do all I can do to make my life meaningful. I tried to finally be the man I watched before I made all of the bad choices that I made. My father, as I said, was a hardworking man and was the best provider, so I didn't get the chance to be the father that my father was to me with my son, although I did the very best that I could with my four daughters. I had a couple of learning experiences with marriages and took something to do, and things not to do. I took Ross' advice, and I didn't give up on love. I married the love of my life, Mrs. Sylvia Weathers, and I have additions to my family. I started telling myself to get rid of all the guilt things and now they are in the rear-view mirror. When I tell you I have found my soul mate that's what I did, and this is the same girl that I met at my friend, Richard's party. She had eyes for me, but it would take a little time, but she would be the first woman in my life that I saw as a partner and not a possession. "

MY BEST FRIEND- MY WIFE

I mean for the first time in my life, I really got to know a woman and it wasn't motivated by sex. I have had many good women; they just had a boy, not a man, and they manipulated and guarded my heart. So, I was always who they thought they wanted but really had no clue who I was; hell, I didn't really know. Now I was drug-free for seventeen years and had at least three (3) women who I was in relationships with all at the same time, but yet I was lonely. There was a hole, I woke up from a bad nightmare and looked to the left and there was a person there, but she wasn't there, I was just on a sex binge. My sponsor told me, "That it was not what I wanted." He suggested, "that I stop hurting women and take some time to get to know myself." After all, I have been living double and triple lifestyles from a very early age and it was time for me to get to know myself and grow up. I had things and was doing all types of legal ways of making money, but there was no happiness in the safe and I deserve to be a good person, someone who could be dependable and a real man, because I had real men as role models and even now, all of these men in my life are real men. I let the little boy out and exposed him. It was time to grow up, so for the first time in my life, I really exposed myself. I went on a date; it was a date. I never did that. Most of the time it was eaten and then sex. Sometimes it was just sex; none of that was working anymore.

Rick told me to go on a date and I tell you it was the best experience. I was close to forty years old and had never really been on a date. This was a real experience and Sylvia made me so comfortable that I revealed exactly who I was to this woman who I barely knew. We sat at the restaurant table and just talked. I mean I was an open book; for once, I was not trying to be manipulative, I just recon honest. I believe she was equally as comfortable because by that time they were letting us know they were about to close. I felt one hundred percent relieved. It was as if I had laid my life out on the table and so did, she. I tell you I didn't know what was going on, but I was free.

I told the truth, so she didn't have to figure out who I was. I told her and I mean everything about me, and I knew her, and we had a connection, and never have we tried to use our past against each other. The truth was we know how to help each other get through our rough times and we also knew our boundaries. Now I know I changed because I have always been possessive and putting my life out, I could now relax. I didn't have to continue living a lifestyle of lies. We dated and I was very attracted to her, but I was hoping that this would go somewhere, so I never worried about sex. I was romancing her, and she was returning the favor. Sylvia became my best friend before my lover and that was the one thing that was missing, just like back in the day. Now I had someone who knew the real Anthony, and she never knew Black, Face, Theo, or any of these people. She only knew Anky and he wasn't such a bad guy. She fell in love with Anthony, the man who had started working on himself, wanting to put the past in the past. I have done my best from the first day until this day. I made her happy and I remain humble. She is my soul mate. I have been a part of a lot of things from the bad to the good. I have made amends and some things I just don't do, but one thing is for sure, I am a straight-up type of guy. My word is my everything! I replaced hate with love, and my desire is to travel and that is something that Sylvia and I do as much as we possibly can. By the way, we are happily married as I write. We have been married for six (6) years and I love her today as much as I ever have. I stay close to Vincent or Eugene; some call him Macho or Box and my two (s) sisters are always checking on me (Delores and Runnett). They are always checking and praying for me. Now, I have been the best father that I know how to be, so I just hope that Carin, Latia, Maegan, and Stephanie know I did my best and for my extended family also. It is a pleasure to be part of all of your lives. It would be out of order not to tell you all that I have another brother, who I really care about, and he sends me the same vibe; Damion is my right-hand man. You see, I have a lot of people who for whatever reason will tell me what I want to hear, but Damion always tells me what I need to hear and that's what I call a real friend. I think by now you should know me, but please don't judge me, I just wanted to share my journey with you!

CONCLUSION

Today, I have been drug-free and a God-fearing man for twenty-seven (27) years. I've been true to my word and done what my angel told me to do. She told me, "To help someone just like she helped me." I have been a Certified Substance Abuse Counselor with the State of Maryland for twenty-five (25) years. I have had the pleasure of helping someone every day, which means I have received help daily. I was hoodwinked by the United States Armed Forces and from that, I still have sleepless nights.

I'm still haunted by the demon, Gunnery Sergeant, but even with all the years of torment, I believe this too shall pass.

I have tried to be the very best husband, father, brother, and friend that I can be. Life has really presented me with challenges, but I am ever so grateful, and I thank God for his Grace and Mercy. I pray that everyone who read this will be able to see that the worst can become the best, just stay the course of your journey and "Remember Me."

DEDICATION

I would like to dedicate this book to my mother, Ora Weathers, my father, Moses Weathers, and a special thanks to my Uncle Esau Weathers.

May they all rest in peace and thanks for making me the person I am.

And my wife

Sylvia Weathers my best friend who always has my back and encourages me to be the best me.

COMING SOON

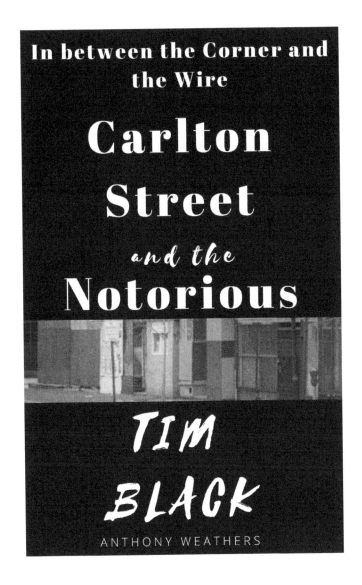

In between the Corner and the Wire

Carlton Street

and the

Notorious

TIM

BLACK

ANTHONY WEATHERS

Made in the USA
Middletown, DE
30 August 2022